*The Book of Amazing Stories*

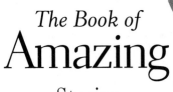

# The Book of
# Amazing
## Stories

*90 Devotions on*
Seeing God's Hand
*in Unlikely Places*

## Robert Petterson

TYNDALE
**MOMENTUM**™

*The nonfiction imprint of*
*Tyndale House Publishers, Inc.*

Visit Tyndale online at www.tyndale.com.

Visit Tyndale Momentum online at www.tyndalemomentum.com.

*TYNDALE*, *Tyndale Momentum*, and Tyndale's quill logo are registered trademarks of Tyndale House Publishers, Inc. The Tyndale Momentum logo is a trademark of Tyndale House Publishers, Inc. Tyndale Momentum is the nonfiction imprint of Tyndale House Publishers, Inc., Carol Stream, Illinois.

*The Book of Amazing Stories: 90 Devotions on Seeing God's Hand in Unlikely Places*

For information about special discounts for bulk purchases, please contact Tyndale House Publishers at csresponse@tyndale.com, or call 1-800-323-9400.

ISBN 978-1-4964-2814-1

Printed in China

23   22   21   20   19   18   17
7    6    5    4    3    2    1

*To my beautiful wife,*
*Joyce Anne Petterson, the queen of my story*
*and its most enduring hero*

# Introduction

According to an old Yiddish proverb, "God made man because he loves stories." Indeed, God must love stories: not only is the Bible full of tales of adventure and intrigue and love, but we humans are also full of stories ourselves. Stories have the capacity to touch something deep within us—something that goes beyond mere facts and logic. They have the power to speak the truth to us, to transform us, to remind us that we are not alone, and to inspire us to believe that the impossible is surely possible.

The stories tucked inside these pages are about real people like you and me. These individuals have lived in every historical age and come from every walk of life. Each has left footprints deeply embedded in our world, often in ways that astound. In these stories, you will discover that there are no little people or small places.

Some stories will ignite your imagination. Others will

catch you by surprise as you learn amazing things you never knew about people you thought you knew. In each one, you will see God's hand at work in the most unexpected places.

In the ninety days ahead, you will find a new story each day to recharge your spiritual batteries. Each entry ends with a thought-provoking principle as well as an accompanying Bible verse to carry you through the day.

It is my hope that these stories will amaze, inspire, and encourage you as much as they have me. History, after all, is really *his* story. The stories in this book prove that each person's story is his—and so is yours. Maybe, as you read, you'll discover that the great Storyteller is weaving together a wonderful story in your own life as well.

*Dr. Robert Petterson*

# The Woman Who Tore down the Wall

⊷⊶

History books will never tell you that Nellie Clyde Wilson ended the Cold War. But history often overlooks its most important people.

Nellie was a little wisp of a woman, born the youngest of seven kids in a small town on the road to nowhere. Despite her strict Presbyterian upbringing, she fell head over heels in love with a dashing Irish Catholic named Jack.

It wasn't long after the wedding that Jack began to show his true colors. Brought up in a family of hard drinkers, Jack had a taste for whiskey. Jobs were hard to come by, and it didn't help that Jack's drunkenness got him repeatedly fired. Their family was forced to move at least ten times in fourteen years. Nellie eked out a meager living by taking in sewing and laundry, and somehow managed to make the meals stretch for Jack and their two boys. Most months she barely scraped together the rent money. Yet she never lost her sense of humor or optimism. Her youngest boy often recalled that she was the most positive woman in his life.

Mostly, her boys observed the way she loved Jesus. They went with her to the jailhouse, bringing hot food to prisoners. They watched her subsist on crackers because she had taken her meal next door to a sick neighbor. When Jack complained about her tithing to the church, Nellie good-naturedly replied that God would make their ninety percent twice as big if he got his tenth.

Nellie was a bit player in small-town America. You might never have known who she was if it hadn't been for her sons. They flourished under her unbounded optimism and grew strong observing her heroic faith. She steeled them with discipline and lavished them with love. Every night she read her boys stories about good and evil. Her youngest son's favorite was about a knight in shining armor who conquered an evil empire. From Nellie, this little boy learned how to dream big and overcome impossible odds. She nurtured his love for acting and told him that he could change the world. Most of all, she taught him to love God.

The world remembers this wisp of a woman by her married name: Nellie (Nelle) Clyde Wilson Reagan. The son she nicknamed Dutch grew up to live out his mother's bedtime story, becoming the knight in shining armor who triumphed over an evil empire. President Ronald Reagan often said that his mother was the most influential person in his life.

Could it be that this diminutive washerwoman from a small town in Illinois was the one who tore down the Berlin

Wall and set millions free from Communist tyranny because of a dream that she instilled in her son?

As you ponder your own life story, you might take heart from something that Nellie wrote in her well-worn Bible:

*You can be too big for God to use, but you can never be too small.*

———✦———

> He gives grace generously. As the Scriptures say,
> "God opposes the proud but gives
> grace to the humble."

JAMES 4:6

# A Mouse That Roared

⌘

H e hated the name that his missionary mother gave him at birth. As a runt fighting for a spot on the rugby fields, he figured that *Henry* was a sissy's name. But it wasn't as bad as the nickname his classmates gave him: the Mouse.

After college, the Mouse returned to China to teach chemistry at a boys' school. When bloody civil war broke out, he went where the fighting was fiercest. His wife begged him not to go, but he was determined to go to those in greatest need. When the Japanese later invaded China, the Mouse sent his family to Canada but refused to leave his mission. It wasn't long before he landed in a concentration camp. He was a quiet hero in that barbed-wire mission field before a brain tumor threatened his life. Winston Churchill pleaded with the Japanese to release him. But when the prisoner exchange took place, the Mouse gave up his spot to a pregnant woman. Not long after, he died in that Japanese camp.

Why was this prisoner so important that the British prime minister personally intervened for his release? Perhaps Churchill recalled a day twenty years earlier when the Mouse roared on the center stage of Olympic history. In 1924 Henry was known by his middle name, Eric. Sportswriters called him the Flying Scotsman. You might have watched his inspiring story in the Oscar-winning film *Chariots of Fire*. At the Paris Olympics he won a gold medal. But a number of Olympians did that in 1924.

The Mouse made headlines for another reason: he refused to run when he discovered that the qualifying heats for his races were set for Sunday. Raised a strict Presbyterian, he believed that it was a sin to compete in athletics on the Sabbath. So the Mouse decided that standing on principle trumped running for gold. When the British Olympic committee pleaded with him to run for king and country, he refused to budge. His stand seems quaintly old-fashioned in an age where sports dominate our Sundays.

The Mouse went to church while others competed. He lost two gold medals but gained the respect of the world for his unwavering integrity. Later that week, he did win a gold medal, setting a world record that stood for a decade. Could it be that this principled stand in Paris produced a hero in China twenty years later? Maybe it was his character as much as his athletic prowess that led to a 2002 poll naming him Scotland's most popular sports figure of all time.

Mice can roar like lions when there's conviction in their bellies. A single mouse standing its ground has been known to stampede bull elephants. You might not agree with Henry Eric Liddell's views on the Sabbath, but in an age of compromise his story is worth remembering. There are some principles that far outweigh gold medals. Certainly this much is true:

*If you don't stand for something, you will fall for anything.*

∽೦಄ல∾

Wide is the gate and broad is the road that leads to destruction, and many enter through it. But small is the gate and narrow the road that leads to life, and only a few find it.

MATTHEW 7:13-14, NIV

# The Triumph of Bubbles

⟨◦⟨◦⟩◦⟩

When Belle Silverman was born with bubbles in her mouth, her immigrant mother gave her a nickname that lasted a lifetime. Yet life was anything but bubbly for the girl called Bubbles. Brooklyn neighbors exclaimed that her golden curls and precocious talent made her a Jewish Shirley Temple. Those compliments became a curse when her obsessive stage mom stole Bubbles's childhood by dragging her to endless auditions for roles in radio, movies, and vaudeville. Mrs. Silverman was sure that her Shirley Temple look-alike was their ticket out of poverty. Repeated rejections at those auditions traumatized little Bubbles. So did the look of disappointment in her mother's eyes.

When she was sixteen, her voice teacher said that she was tailor made for the opera. But nothing ever came easy for Bubbles. She spent ten frustrating years on the road trying to make it in second-tier operas. The New York City Opera turned her down seven times before they accepted her. When Bubbles finally snagged a starring role, critics panned her performances as uneven. Leading opera houses refused to let her appear on their stages. It was only after she went to

Europe and won over the toughest opera fans in the world that critics begrudgingly recognized her magnificent voice.

Even when she became a star at the Met and *Time* magazine dubbed her America's Queen of the Opera, her adoring public never knew that Bubbles was raising two children with disabilities. One of them was severely cognitively disabled. She spent a fortune building a sanctuary for her kids in Martha's Vineyard. After they moved in, it burned to the ground. Then her husband collapsed with a stroke. She cared for him for eight years while raising two children with special needs and juggling a demanding career.

You might think that a lifetime of setbacks would make Belle Silverman from Crown Heights a sour woman. But the lady nicknamed Bubbles plowed through her troubles with infectious joy. Barbara Walters called her the happiest person on earth. After a *Sixty Minutes* interview, Mike Wallace said that she was the most impressive person he had ever met. When he asked her how she had overcome bitterness to be so bubbly, she replied, "I can't control the circumstances of my life, but I can choose to be joyful."

You may remember Belle Silverman by her stage name, Beverly Sills. When Belle died in 2007, a *New York Times* obituary proclaimed the Brooklyn-born coloratura soprano to be America's most popular opera star since Enrico Caruso. But to family and friends, she will always remain Bubbles. Two years before her death, she summed up her challenges and triumphs to a *Times* reporter: "Man plans, and God laughs. I've never considered myself a happy woman. How could I be with all that's happened to me? But I choose to be a cheerful woman." When you face speed bumps on life's road, it might help to recall this line from Bubbles:

***Circumstances are often beyond your choice, but you can choose to be cheerful.***

———— ✦ ————

Worry weighs a person down; an
encouraging word cheers a person up.

PROVERBS 12:25

# The Man of a Million Lies

⋰◌◌◌⋰

His Italian mother named him after Saint Mark in the hopes that he would always tell the gospel truth. Yet when he later wrote a bestseller about his travels, cynics called it a book of a million lies. He was nicknamed Mark of a Million Lies.

In the 1200s, Europeans found it impossible to believe Mark's tales of a twenty-four-year odyssey that took him across the steppes of Russia, over mountains in Afghanistan, through deserts in Persia, and around the Himalayas into the far reaches of Asia.

Mark was one of the first Europeans to enter China. Through amazing circumstances, he became a favorite of the most powerful man on earth. Kublai Khan ruled over a domain that eclipsed the ancient Roman Empire. Mark saw cities that made Western capitals look like roadside villages. The khan's palace dwarfed the largest cathedrals and castles in Europe. It was so massive that its banquet hall could seat six thousand guests, all dining on plates of pure gold. He saw the world's first paper money and marveled at the explosive power of gunpowder. It would be five hundred years before

Europe would produce as much steel as China manufactured in 1267, and six hundred years before the Pony Express would equal the speed of Kublai Khan's postal service.

Mark began his journey home to Venice loaded down with gold, silk, and spices. According to some accounts, tucked away in his pocket was a recipe for that Chinese culinary delight, pasta. The khan had sent him on his way with a royal guard of one thousand men. By the time they reached the Indian Ocean, six hundred had drowned or died of disease. A ragged Mark barely limped home, most of his riches lost along the way.

Folks dismissed his stories, and it wasn't long before he landed in jail. In that lonely dungeon, he dictated his fantastic yarns to a writer of romance novels. Those stories were marketed as *The Travels of Marco Polo*. But a skeptical public dismissed it as a book of a million lies.

Mark got out of that prison and went on to make another fortune. Yet he never shook that moniker, Marco the Liar. As he lay on his deathbed, his family, friends, and parish priest implored him to recant his fabrications lest they land him in hell. Mark spit out his final words: "I have not even told you half of what I saw."

Medieval cynics dismissed his stories as the tall tales of a lunatic or a liar. Yet history has established the credibility of *The Travels of Marco Polo*. A century later, another Italian read Mark's stories. By the time Christopher Columbus finished them, a dream was sparked that he, too, could discover new worlds.

Is there anything sadder than folks who are afraid to dream big or explore new worlds? Don't you dare be one of them! Allow Mark's story to send you out today with a sense of excitement, keeping this in mind:

***You haven't seen the half of all the wonders that are still out there.***

———— ∞ ————

Eye has not seen, nor ear heard, nor have entered the heart of man the things which God has prepared for those who love Him.

1 CORINTHIANS 2:9, NKJV

# When Faith Walked across Niagara Falls

⌘

Niagara Falls is some kind of monster. Less than a handful of daredevils have challenged its fury and lived to tell about it. It's no wonder that more than one hundred thousand spectators gathered there and millions more tuned in to ABC to watch Nik Wallenda's death-defying aerial feat.

Nothing was left to chance in June of 2012. A 1,800-foot-long, two-inch-thick steel cable weighing seven tons was pulled across the falls by machines, stretched taut, and then secured by bolts driven deep into bedrock. Supporting cables were attached to the main wire to make sure it couldn't sway. The aerial artist wore the latest high-tech clothing and shoes. His sponsors required that he wear a harness that tethered him safely to the high wire. Protected by all these precautions, Wallenda completed the walk to the delight of the crowd, ABC television, his corporate sponsors, and his nervous family.

If only you could have been there on June 30, 1859. This time the daredevil was the Great Blondin. His aerial acrobatics had thrilled audiences across the world. Yet Niagara

Falls would be the Frenchman's greatest challenge. Blondin didn't take the same precautions that Nik Wallenda would take some 150 years later. Instead of a steel cable, he walked on a two-inch-thick Manila rope. No machines pulled it taut, and no cables held it steady. He refused to wear a safety harness. Instead of high-tech gear, he donned Turkish pantaloons and Persian slippers. He carried a wooden pole five times heavier than Wallenda's. Because his high wire was a 1,300-foot stretch of rope, Blondin walked downhill to the middle, some fifty feet below where he began, and back uphill to the end.

Wallenda performed his aerial extravaganza once. Blondin did his daredevil feats repeatedly over two summers, each time doing something more stupefying. He crossed that Manila rope on a bicycle, on stilts, and in the pitch black of night. Once he pushed a stove on a wheelbarrow and cooked an omelet high over the falls. On another occasion he climbed into a gunnysack blindfolded and then shuffled across that rope. As amazing as Wallenda's *one* feat might have seemed in 2012, Blondin's many stunts were far more electrifying in 1859.

But history mostly recalls that day when he asked ten thousand spectators if they believed that he could carry a man on his shoulders across Niagara Falls. The crowd responded with a roar of affirmation. He retorted, "Who then will get up on my back?" No one moved. So Blondin turned to his manager, Harry Colcord, and ordered him to climb up on his shoulders. Colcord was petrified, but he had promoted the Frenchman too long to back down. He later said that his half-hour ride on Blondin's shoulders was an eternity of terror.

Faith is not a spectator sport. It's one thing to experience adventure vicariously through someone else's high-risk faith. It's quite another to walk the high wire yourself. Today God may call you to climb on his shoulders and cross over some scary place. If so, something Corrie ten Boom wrote might help:

*Never be afraid to trust an unknown future to a known God.*

———— ✦ ————

Now faith is confidence in what we hope for
and assurance about what we do not see.

HEBREWS 11:1, NIV

# A Shoemaker Who Changed the World

౼౷౦౷౼

Willie was a stuttering plodder. The only job he could get was as a shoemaker's apprentice. The only girl who would marry him was Dorothy, who suffered from mental illness. But everything changed for Willie when he read a runaway bestseller. Most who read Captain Cook's journal were captivated by the exploits of a daring explorer. But Willie saw vast human needs in faraway places. He fashioned a world globe from leather scraps. After staring at it, he sobbed, "Here am I, Lord. Send me!"

Protestants were not sending foreign missionaries in the 1700s. When Willie stammered out his vision at a meeting of Calvinistic Baptists, an old pastor angrily shouted, "Young man, sit down! When God pleases to convert the heathen, he will do it without you or me!" Others tried to dissuade Willie by reminding him that he was a shoemaker saddled with a crazy wife. Someone said, "Face it, William: you're unfit." He stuttered, "B-b-but I c-c-can p-p-plod!"

For the next eleven years, Willie plodded until he could read the Bible in Latin, Greek, Dutch, and French. He was finally licensed to preach. When he wasn't in the pulpit of his tiny church, he rode across England, stuttering a message: "Expect great things from God. Attempt great things for God." Fortified by that credo, he gathered like-minded pastors to establish the Baptist Mission Society. He was so poor that he couldn't contribute a single penny to his new venture.

Yet he managed to collect a handful of missionaries and some pitiful resources to go to India. In 1793 they might as well have been going to the moon. His wife sat on the dock, refusing to leave. Twice Willie had to get on his knees and beg her to board the ship. When the missionaries arrived in India, Hindu radicals tried to kill them. The British East India Company refused to let them travel inland. Willie's five-year-old son died, and Dorothy lost her mind completely.

Willie labored seven years before he saw his first conversion. After twenty years, he had only a handful of converts. His first wife died, and then his second. But he continued to plod. When he died in 1834 at age seventy-three, he had translated the Bible into thirty-four languages, founded India's first college, established forty-five teaching centers, alleviated famine by teaching new agricultural methods, and worked to free Indian women from the cruelest sorts of bondage.

If you visit India today, you can find Willie's statue close to the parliament building. Even Hindus celebrate him as one of their nation's greatest heroes. History recalls Willie by his full name, William Carey. He has been dubbed the Father of Modern Missions. But he would be more impressed to know that some 25 million people in India have called Jesus Christ their Savior, and today there are five times more Christians in India than in England. Maybe you're just a plodder like Willie, in a place as small as a village cobbler's shop. Yet as long as you can plod, you can do so much more, if only you do what he did:

*Expect great things from God. Attempt great things for God.*

---

I am the LORD, the God of all the peoples of the world. Is anything too hard for me?

JEREMIAH 32:27

# The Day the Music Died

e⊚⊚⊚৩

*R*olling *Stone* magazine called his suicide "the day the music died." He might not have become a hostile loner who hated authority if his parents hadn't turned his childhood home into a war zone. Yet this alienated teen found his escape in a cast-off guitar that unlocked his genius. His blistering music, raw lyrics, and angry performances introduced a new word to the pop lexicon: *grunge*. By 1993 his band had recorded two megahit albums. Its signature song, "Smells Like Teen Spirit," became the anthem of Generation X.

Kurt was now the biggest rock star on the planet. Yet he couldn't shake the angst of a tortured childhood. While he screamed at the world, painful stomach spasms shrieked back at him. When prescription drugs didn't work, he shot up heroin to kill the pain. In an attempt to create the family he never knew as a child, he got married. But his rocker wife was also hooked on heroin, and they fought as viciously as his parents had—until the baby came.

Kurt said that his daughter was the only pure thing in his life. Then his wife confessed in a *Vanity Fair* interview that she used heroin during her pregnancy. Kurt just about lost his mind fighting legal battles to keep authorities from taking his child. His screaming fits with his band, Nirvana, became tabloid fodder. After he almost died of an overdose in Italy, he returned to Seattle and locked himself in a room with loaded guns. His wife called 911, and police raided his estate.

By now his wife was running scared. She flew to Los Angeles to kick her drug habit, and begged Kurt to do the same for their baby's sake. He checked himself into a clinic where a psychiatrist said that he was a seething volcano, re-living his childhood traumas as if they had just happened. When he got out, he promised to let go of the past. He flew home to Seattle, locked himself in his guesthouse, and took his own life.

When the news hit the media, teens across America locked themselves in their bedrooms. MTV said that Nirvana was to the 90s what the Beatles had been to the 60s, and Kurt Cobain's suicide was as catastrophic as John Lennon's murder. *Rolling Stone* magazine declared him the voice of a lost generation.

Kurt had so much to live for. Within ten years he sold 50 million albums. Nirvana was the flagship of Generation X. Fans worldwide were ready to make its next album another megahit. *Rolling Stone* ranked him the twelfth best guitarist of all time, and MTV listed him as the seventh greatest singer in pop history. In 2006 he surpassed Elvis as the top-selling deceased celebrity, and in 2014 he was elected to the Rock and Roll Hall of Fame. Weep for the troubled superstar who couldn't let go of past resentments. As you begin your new year, allow this lesson from Kurt's story to be a springboard for success:

*No one ever moved forward while chained to the past.*

꠸꠸

But one thing I do: forgetting what lies behind
and straining forward to what lies ahead,
I press on toward the goal for the prize of
the upward call of God in Christ Jesus.

PHILIPPIANS 3:13-14, ESV

# The Day an Angel Fed Angels

⚬⚬⚬

Jaye was the child of a poor Southern family, growing up in a ramshackle house on a country dirt road. Times were tough, and food was in short supply.

She was playing in the yard on a hot summer day when she heard the clanging of chains. She looked up to see grizzled men dressed in black-and-white-striped uniforms shackled together and shuffling down the road. Two armed guards led the chain gang to a shade tree where they all sat down.

One of the guards knocked on the front door and asked Jaye's mother if his men could get a drink of water from the backyard pump. She agreed, but there was a look of concern as she pulled her girl into the house. Jaye watched from a window as prisoners were unchained one by one to hobble over and drink. After they quenched their thirst, guards and prisoners retreated to the shade.

Jaye's mother called her to the kitchen. In the blink of an eye, she had ferreted out the final tins of tuna in the cupboard. She used the last bread in the house to make a tray of tuna fish sandwiches. Alongside them stood two pitchers of ice-cold lemonade. She passed one pitcher to Jaye, and then, lifting the tray of sandwiches and the other pitcher, she led her out of the house and across the road.

Guards and prisoners began to stand up. But Jaye's mother said, "Oh no! Stay where you are! I'll serve you." With little Jaye at her side, she went down the line, filling each convict's tin cup with lemonade and giving each man a sandwich. A white woman serving lunch to black convicts on a chain gang was no small thing in the Deep South more than fifty years ago.

Each man silently ate his tuna fish sandwich and savored a tin cup of lemonade. Jaye remembers a quiet reverence like that in a cathedral. As the prisoners got up, one man said to Jaye's mother, "Ma'am, I've wondered all my life if I'd ever see an angel, and now I have. Thank you!" She softly replied, "You are all welcome. God bless you!" The prisoners moved on, their steps a bit quicker and their shoulders a little higher. Jaye never saw them again. But she remembers her mother mumbling a Bible verse about entertaining angels.

Jaye Lewis has grown up to be a wonderful writer of short stories. She still can't recall what her mother managed to scrape together from an almost empty cupboard to feed her own family that night. Some fifty years later, she knows one thing for sure: the same angel who served that chain gang served her family that night. Jaye's mother would disagree. She would quickly say that the real angel was more likely one of those prisoners. We never know when angels might drop by our house. They seldom look the way we picture them. Remember the story of Jaye Lewis's mother as you interact with others today. You might want to repeat this to yourself with each encounter:

*I could be a person serving an angel, or like an angel serving people.*

———— ∞ ————

Don't forget to show hospitality to strangers, for some who have done this have entertained angels without realizing it!

HEBREWS 13:2

# A Map to Nowhere

❧

Losing your way can be fatal. George found that out the hard way. This dirt-poor farmer, with dreams of striking it rich, was in Springfield, Illinois, the day fast-talking James Reed held a crowd spellbound with tales of fabulous riches in California. Reed ended with a rousing challenge: "Come on, boys! You can have as much land as you want without it costing you anything."

Reed's promise of free land would cost everything for those who followed him, including George and his family. A lineup of wagons rolled out of Independence, Missouri, and by the time they arrived in Fort Laramie, they were already behind schedule. It was now July, and the wagons still had to cross a brutal stretch of mountains and badlands before winter set in. That's when Reed pulled out a book with a map that promised to cut some four hundred miles off the route to California, even though its author had never seen the trail. Neither had anyone else. Reed's map was based on rumor and legend. Frontiersmen warned that it was a fraud. But Reed convinced eighty-six people to join him. George was among those most enthusiastic. Maybe that's why the group elected him as their captain.

Their gamble proved disastrous. Heavy wagons had to be dragged over the rugged Wasatch Mountains and then across the Great Salt Lake Desert. By the time George's party found their way back to the California Trail, it was the end of September. Their "shortcut" had taken twenty-five days longer than the normal route. Weeks behind schedule and short on food, they reached California in late October.

The weary party might have made it up that last stretch of the Sierra Nevada Mountains had they not been hit by a freak blizzard. It was the first in a series of massive snowstorms leading to the worst winter in California history. The marooned party ate the last of their oxen, only to face five more months trapped. A desperate group, calling themselves the Forlorn Hope, set out for Fort Sutter on crudely fashioned snowshoes. Less than half of them made it.

Four search parties were turned back by blizzards before a handful of survivors were finally rescued in the spring of 1847. The rescuers were appalled to discover the grisly remains of half-eaten corpses. The survivors confessed that they had stayed alive by eating the frozen bodies of the dead. These reports of cannibalism became the fodder for sensational newspaper stories across a horrified nation.

George was not one of those eaten. But it would have only been a matter of time. This dreamer and schemer was found dead and half-frozen on his bed. Some 165 years later, history still recoils in horror at George's last name, Donner. His notorious name is indelibly etched in the history of the Old West. The bizarre story of the Donner Party is a sobering reminder of what can happen when people opt for the shortcut. The promise of a faster and easier way often leads to long delays. Bestselling author Orrin Woodward makes a lot of sense when he says this:

*There are many shortcuts to failure, but no shortcuts to true success.*

༄༅

There is a way which seems right to a man, but in the end it leads to death.

PROVERBS 14:12, WEB

# The World's Most-Admired Woman

⁓⁕⁓

No one would have ever guessed that scrawny little Agnes would one day light up the world. Like most folks in her poverty-stricken eastern-European country, she seemed doomed to a dead-end life. After her widowed mother had exhausted herself trying to find an eligible bachelor for the mousy girl, Agnes announced that God had called her to be a missionary. Everyone said she was crazy. But eighteen-year-old Agnes headed for the faraway city of Dublin, Ireland. After learning a smattering of English, she moved to Asia where she kicked around from school to school, seemingly consigned to teach schoolchildren forever.

Everything changed when Agnes went on a spiritual retreat to a nearby city. There she stumbled upon the worst slums on earth. She was overwhelmed by the poverty and disease. At thirty-six years of age, the diminutive spinster heard Jesus tell her to bring his light to this place of darkness. She called other women to join her in ministering to the poorest outcasts in India.

The world doesn't know her as Agnes: after she committed

herself to ministry, she changed her name to the patron saint of missionaries, Teresa. Who would have figured that the Gallup Poll would one day declare this pint-size Albanian woman the most admired woman of the twentieth century? Or that she would win the Nobel Prize? Or that her order would grow to 4,500 sisters in 153 countries giving themselves to the poorest of the poor? Who would believe that from her one-room cell in a Calcutta convent, she would oversee a worldwide string of hospitals, hospices, AIDS centers, orphanages, and schools?

When Mother Teresa won the Nobel Prize, reporters asked her how we should promote world peace. She shocked everyone with her simple answer: "Go home and love your family." When they asked her to describe herself, she replied, "By blood, I am an Albanian; by citizenship, an Indian; by faith, a Catholic nun. As to my calling, I belong to the world. As to my heart, I belong entirely to Jesus."

When a delegation of nuns came to Calcutta to discover the secret to Mother Teresa's success, the head of one order asked, "Why are you growing while so many other orders are dying?"

Mother Teresa quietly replied, "I give them Jesus."

"I know that," replied the woman impatiently. "But can you be more specific? Do your sisters object to wearing habits? What about the rules of your order? How do you enforce them?"

"Only one thing matters. I give them Jesus," she replied again.

"Yes, yes, I know that!" persisted the woman. "But there's got to be more than that!"

The little nun walked up to the woman and said in the sternest voice possible, "I give them Jesus! There's nothing more!"

Jesus alone can change the world. By giving Jesus only, even a humble nun from a hardscrabble upbringing can change the world. So can we, if we remember this from Agnes's story:

*Religion does not save or transform people. Only Jesus does.*

⸻ ↝⊙↜ ⸻

But we all, with unveiled face, beholding as in a
mirror the glory of the Lord, are being transformed
into the same image from glory to glory.

2 CORINTHIANS 3:18, NKJV

# The Man of a Thousand Faces

⟡

N o one could play someone else better than Richard. Born into a vaudeville family, he began performing onstage while still a toddler. By the time he was a teenager, he was a master impressionist who could transform himself into a variety of characters. But it was at home that Richard honed the fine art of the masquerade. Dominated by an overprotective mother, he learned to play whatever role made her happy. By the time he was an adult, Richard didn't know who he was anymore. Maybe that's why he plowed through four marriages and his children complained that they never really knew their father.

Who would have guessed that this master impressionist and comic genius was lost and miserable? Toward the end of a brilliant career spanning sixty films, Richard was interviewed by Kermit the Frog on *The Muppet Show*. The puppet said, "Just relax and be yourself."

Richard responded, "I can't be myself, because I don't know who I really am anymore."

After years of cardiac trouble brought on by anxiety, alcohol, and drugs, Richard was told that his heart was dying.

Racing against the clock, he tried to mend fences. He confessed to a son that he shouldn't have abandoned his first wife. He deeply regretted alienating his kids. Mostly, he wished he hadn't wasted his life trying to be what others wanted him to be.

Not long after that, Richard collapsed of a heart attack. He was rushed to a London hospital, where he died on July 24, 1980. He was only fifty-four years old. His son Michael tearfully spoke to reporters about the last days that he shared with his dad: "It marked the beginning of an all-too-brief closeness between us."

Michael's dad was born Richard Henry Sellers. But the world remembers him by his screen name, Peter Sellers. He portrayed such memorable characters as Dr. Strangelove and Inspector Clouseau, the bumbling master of disguise in the Pink Panther movies. Before Sellers died, an article in *Time* magazine quoted one of his friends as saying, "Poor Peter! The real Peter disappeared a long time ago. What remains is an amalgamation of all the characters he has played, and he is frantically trying to unsnarl the mess to find out who he really is."

Film critics agree that Peter Sellers was the greatest comedic genius since Charlie Chaplin. No one was funnier than Inspector Clouseau. Nothing is sadder than the story of the actor who played him. His life is summed up in a Smokey Robinson song: "Ain't too much sadder than the tears of a clown when there's no one around. . . . I'm hurt and I want you to know, but for others I put on a show." Hopefully those words aren't your story too. Don't settle for brief moments of closeness such as those Michael shared with his dad at the end. You can experience authentic relationships with those who matter, if you remember this:

*To try to be someone else is to waste the person you were created to be.*

———— ❧ ————

You made all the delicate, inner parts of my body and knit me together in my mother's womb. Thank you for making me so wonderfully complex! Your workmanship is marvelous—how well I know it.

PSALM 139:13-14

# The Treasure of the Salinas de San Andreas

༻⊙⊙⊙༺

When Billy Ford headed across the Guadalupe River, he couldn't have known that he was about to push America to the brink of war. Had the sheriff understood the high stakes that night in 1854, he might have formed a bigger posse than seventeen Americans, ten Mexicans, and an Englishman. He surely needed more firepower than his sixty-four-pound howitzer, especially if he was going to seize the Salinas de San Andreas.

Acre for acre, this was the richest land in Texas, worth its weight in gold. As far back as prehistoric times it had been a bonanza. Aztecs and Mayans traveled great distances to extract its riches. In 1647, a Spanish king granted Don Diego de Vivar exclusive rights to mine its wealth, making his family fabulously wealthy.

By 1854, powerful men were willing to sell their souls to possess the Salinas de San Andreas. But Sheriff Ford should have known better. For more than two hundred years, Comanches, Apaches, Spaniards, Frenchmen, Mexicans, Americans, and Tejanos had fought to the death over this treasure trove of the Trans-Pecos. Somewhere in the badlands of Texas, Ford's outgunned posse ran into an army of Tejanos. After a deadly shoot-out, he hightailed it back to New Mexico.

Some twenty-three years later, this simmering conflict erupted again. Like a scene out of the cowboy comedy *Blazing Saddles*, several small armies converged west of El Paso. Mexican federales crossed the Rio Grande, Apaches rode in from the west, Comanches swooped down from the north, vigilantes stormed out of El Paso, and five hundred Mexican American locals rushed to protect their claim to the Salinas de San Andreas. Just when things couldn't get crazier, hired gunslingers came in by railroad just as Texas rangers arrived from Austin. In the confusion that followed, Tejanos captured Texas rangers, Apaches scalped vigilantes, Comanches shot it out with gunslingers, and federales fled back across the Rio Grande. The Ninth Cavalry, made up of African American buffalo soldiers, finally galloped in to restore order. This fiasco looked like an eye-poking contest between the Three Stooges, but it garnered world headlines and almost caused a war between the United States and Mexico.

What was this treasure that made men crazy with greed? It wasn't gold, oil, or cattle. But it was the richest salt preserve in North America. Unless you hail from West Texas, you have probably never heard about these shoot-outs. After the San Elizario Salt War, America turned to cheaper salt from

Kansas. Today Salinas de San Andreas is a deserted stretch of badlands.

In a day of cheap table salt, it's hard to believe that more wars in history have been fought over salt than have been waged over gold or religion. People can live without gold or oil but not salt. Jesus said, "You are the salt of the earth" (Matthew 5:13). We are to do what salt does: heal, preserve, and bring flavor to life. So get out of the shaker and spread yourself around.

*Salty Christians make others thirst for Jesus, the water of life.*

———— ∞ ————

You are the salt of the earth. But if the salt loses
its saltiness, how can it be made salty again?
It is no longer good for anything, except to
be thrown out and trampled underfoot.

MATTHEW 5:13, NIV

# The Asterisk in an Obituary

⋖⊙⊚⊙⊱

S he was as cute as a button, the first crush for a generation of boys. But the final three years of her twenty-seven-year battle with multiple sclerosis were a waking nightmare. Once the most recognizable teen on the planet, she was now unable to recognize anyone. She existed in a coma-like state, propped up in an electrically controlled chair, nearly blind, unable to speak or go to the bathroom on her own. In those last three years she was fed through a tube. Her throat had to be cleared several times an hour to prevent her from choking to death.

There was a time when she was a pop culture icon. No one received more fan mail than America's favorite Mouseketeer. In 1960, a nationwide poll voted her teenager of the year. Dubbed America's sweetheart, she went on to drive young men crazy in movies like *Beach Blanket Bingo* and *How to Stuff a Wild Bikini*.

She broke hearts across the land when she married her agent in 1965. Even Linus deadpanned in a *Peanuts* cartoon strip, "How depressing . . . Annette Funicello has grown up!" After the wedding, she stepped out of the limelight. But no baby boomer could ever forget the darling of *The Mickey Mouse Club* who became a beach blanket beauty.

Annette began to lose control in her legs when she came out of retirement to do a movie in 1991. A deeply religious woman, she was afraid that people would think she was drunk. So she went public about her MS. America applauded her gutsy battle with this degenerative disease. When she dropped out of sight again, no one knew how much MS was ravaging her. Nor would anyone have recognized her in the end. But her family had a front-row seat to her nightmare. In announcing her death in April of 2013, her children said, "Our mother is now dancing in heaven."

Within a week of Annette's passing, Google recorded millions of hits on her life and death. Almost every article contained a single throwaway line: "In 1986, she married her second husband, horse trainer Glen Holt." Glen was only an asterisk in Annette's obituary.

Few folks know that Annette Funicello's first husband was abusive or that this horse trainer gave her refuge when she had nowhere to go. Within a year of their wedding, she was diagnosed with multiple sclerosis. Yet during those last years, he bathed her, lifted her on and off the toilet, changed her diapers, and attended to her every need. In the end, America's sweetheart was ravaged, bloated, and comatose. It's easy to love the girl of our fantasies, but Glen loved her in dirty diapers and with bloated flesh—not for a while, but for nine thousand straight days.

When asked if it was a burden, he replied, "How can it be when you love somebody?" Maybe you are one of those unsung heroes who is caring for someone. If you're tired and wondering how long you can hang on, know this:

*Anyone can carry a burden to nightfall. Heroes get up and do it again tomorrow.*

———— ✽ ————

Let us not become weary in doing good,
for at the proper time we will reap a
harvest if we do not give up.

GALATIANS 6:9, NIV

# A Letter from the Birmingham Jail

⋘⊚⋙

Who would have believed that Michael would grow up to change the world? Surely the odds were stacked against a black baby born in the Old South. It helped that his preacher daddy saw him as a special gift from God. Maybe that's why this child prodigy entered college at the tender age of fifteen.

But his early success masked the deep scars of segregation. He first felt the sting of the Southern class system when a white friend invited him home. His playmate's mother chased Michael away while loudly berating her son for bringing a "colored boy" into the house. By the time he was a teenager, he no longer trusted a religion that looked the other way while folks practiced bigotry. The preacher's kid dismissed the Bible as myth and rebelled against church.

Everyone was shocked when he announced that he was off to seminary. But Michael didn't enter the ministry so much to preach the gospel as to use his pulpit to promote racial justice. He organized bus boycotts and peaceful protests. When redneck sheriffs unleashed their police dogs, he responded, "Throw us in jail, and we shall still love you. . . . Beat us and leave us half dead, and we shall still love you. But be ye assured that we will wear you down by our capacity to suffer. "

Just when it seemed that Michael's nonviolent protests were finally paying off, the US attorney general ordered an investigation. Secret FBI wiretaps suggested his associations with Communist influences. Agents also uncovered evidence implicating him as a serial adulterer. When his wife found out, she threatened to leave him.

By 1963, many of his impatient followers were deserting to militant groups with slogans like "Burn, baby! Burn!" Michael hit rock bottom when he was thrown into Birmingham City Jail. With plenty of free time, he began to reread the Bible he had dismissed as myth. As he studied letters written by a jailed apostle some 1,900 years earlier, he realized that his hope wasn't in how much he loved others but in how much his Savior loved him.

Not only did Michael experience a conversion in Birmingham, so did the nation. Violent police reaction to his peaceful protests galvanized America. Not long after, he was awarded the Nobel Peace Prize. The name Michael appears on his birth certificate, but history remembers the moniker that his preacher daddy later gave him: Martin. By the time he was assassinated in 1968, Dr. Martin Luther King Jr. had unleashed a tidal wave that changed everything.

Every February the United States celebrates his birthday. But maybe you don't feel like throwing a party, because you still feel the sting of bigotry. Perhaps you are imprisoned in your own jailhouse, shackled to the ball and chain of some disability or disappointment. Could it be that, like Martin, you are deeply aware of your own hidden flaws and failures? Take heart. You just might find courage from a line that Dr. King penned in that Birmingham jail:

*You must accept finite disappointment, but never lose infinite hope.*

---

And we know that in all things God works
for the good of those who love him, who have
been called according to his purpose.

ROMANS 8:28, NIV

# The Song of a Human Trafficker

౸ఄఄఄఄౚ

Johnny was a latchkey kid. His mother had died, and his father was a ship's captain off at sea. Abandoned and adrift, he roamed the streets as a pickpocket and trouble-maker. When Johnny's sea captain father returned, he took eleven-year-old Johnny aboard his ship, figuring that the rough life of a sailor might knock some sense into his prodigal son. Instead, his boy became even more unruly, creating mayhem in almost every port of call.

His disgusted father finally gave him his walking papers. Johnny signed on to another vessel where he attempted desertion by jumping ship. He was captured by the shore patrol and publicly flogged. When the word got around that the ship captain's son was incorrigible, no respectable vessel would sign him on. So Johnny became a deckhand aboard a slave ship, hauling human cargo to the Americas.

Just when it seemed that he couldn't sink any lower, Johnny was enslaved by a man named Amos Clow, whose African mistress took special delight in having a white slave as her personal plaything. After he escaped, he was possessed with an implacable hatred for Africans. When he became the captain of his own slave ship, his brutality knew no bounds.

It took a violent storm to mark the beginning of change in his life. On a return trip to England, when it seemed that his ship was about to sink, Johnny cried out to Jesus for salvation. It took a few more years for this new convert to quit the slave business, yet God was slowly transforming his racist heart.

Eventually, Johnny felt called to the pulpit. The archbishop of York rejected him because his past was too scandalous. Finally, he was given a small parish. But curious crowds came to hear this notorious slave trader turned preacher. He wrote almost three hundred hymns to accompany his sermons. Eight years after he became a pastor, Johnny penned history's most famous hymn, "Amazing Grace."

A single line in the first stanza jumps off the page: "Amazing grace, how sweet the sound, that saved a wretch like me." Surely, the Reverend John Newton knew firsthand the power of sin to reduce humans to utter wretchedness. When he later wrote a pamphlet on the slave trade, his exposé on the wretchedness of human trafficking helped bring about the abolition of slavery in the British Empire three decades before America's Civil War.

Over the past several years many hymnals have replaced the term "wretch" in "Amazing Grace" with words that are less offensive to a culture obsessed with positive self-image.

But maybe we lose something of the grandeur of God's grace when we minimize our own sinful condition. To take the "wretch" out of "Amazing Grace" is to cut the very heart out of a hymn celebrating the immensity of God's love for us. Old Johnny Newton might even say this:

*Take the wretch out of "Amazing Grace," and you take the amazing out of grace.*

———— ✺ ————

But God is so rich in mercy, and he loved us so much, that even though we were dead because of our sins, he gave us life when he raised Christ from the dead. (It is only by God's grace that you have been saved!)

EPHESIANS 2:4-5

# The Chambermaid's Choice

⌘

Maria had hoped that her second marriage would make for a better future. Though born the daughter of a cook, she had dreams of being in high society. But at sixteen, she fell madly in love with a nobleman's valet. When they married, she consigned herself to be dismissed as one of the serving class. After Maria gave birth to a son, her valet husband died. At age eighteen she was a grieving widow and a single mother. Not long after, her little boy died too.

Then she got a second chance at love. But when her young musician took her home to meet his prominent family, they looked down their haughty noses at this girl from the serving class. His father would ever after refer to her as "the chambermaid." Her husband's family would always view her as an inferior interloper. It was no wonder that Maria's second marriage soon soured.

She later referred to her life as "a chain of sorrows." The couple's first child died six days after he was born. The "chambermaid" would bury five of her eight children. But her worst heartache was watching the decline of a husband who enjoyed the tavern more than practicing his music. If he wasn't in a drunken stupor, he was with other women. Then the beatings began. After he took advantage of her in one of his brutal rages, Maria discovered she was pregnant. She determined that she wasn't about to bring a child conceived by rape into her miserable world.

She found her way to a woman who traded in concoctions that induced miscarriage. Three drops of that deadly liquid would kill her baby. Any more might end her life too. She dumped it all into a cup of tea. But before she was able to drink it, the cup was accidentally knocked off the table. At first she was hysterical. Then she resigned herself to the fact that God must have a purpose for her unwanted child.

He turned out to be a strange little boy, often reclusive and unresponsive. But he did have his family's love for music. When a local teacher took him on as a piano student, no one imagined that she was gaining a prodigy. Maria was forty years old when Wolfgang Mozart allegedly declared that her son was destined for greatness. Two months later, the teenage prodigy rushed home to be at her deathbed. She told her son that giving birth to him was the best thing she ever did in her unhappy life.

We should all be grateful that Maria van Beethoven did not abort little Ludwig, a child of rape who would grow up to write the world's greatest symphonies. Maybe you, too, were unplanned or unwanted. But God conceived you as his masterpiece. Perhaps you are facing a tough choice or difficult circumstances. Answers never come easily in times like these. Hopefully Maria's story and that of her unwanted child, Ludwig van Beethoven, might give you courage to do this:

*Trust God. He knows who belongs in your life and who doesn't.*

❧

I was thrust into your arms at my birth. You have been my God from the moment I was born.

PSALM 22:10

# The Fifteen-Minute Superstar

⌒⊙⊙⌒

Hardly anyone remembers Jamie Foss, or the television show that gave her fifteen minutes of dubious fame. The program aired in 2004 with auditions held across the nation. Contestants were chosen by three celebrity judges and then flown to Hollywood to take part in a nationally televised competition. Each contestant was given vocal coaching, makeovers, and critiques of their performances. The grand prize was a recording contract, along with the promise of becoming America's next superstar. Week after week, singers were eliminated until a winner was crowned on the final episode.

If you are thinking *American Idol* or *The Voice*, you are wrong. Its name was much more grandiose: *Superstar USA*. But its premise was the polar opposite of those other televised competitions. Three celebrity judges intentionally eliminated anyone who had any talent, while praising outrageously bad performances and advancing the worst singers to the next round.

The judges and those who tuned in to *Superstar USA* were laughing at these wannabes with inflated egos. The premise of the show was that you could never go wrong banking on people's capacity for self-delusion. The Danish philosopher Søren Kierkegaard was right when he wrote, "There are two ways to be fooled: one is to believe what isn't so; the other is to refuse to believe what is so."

The final contestants performed in front of a live audience. By now the judges had winnowed the group down to the worst singers. The producers deceived the studio audience by saying that the performers were terminally ill teens whose last wish was to perform in front of a live television audience. Compassionate spectators gave standing ovations to some of the ghastliest performances in the history of American television.

At the end of the final show, judges chose the worst performer and crowned her the winner. Jamie was overwhelmed with joy at being crowned Superstar USA. But her exuberance was short lived. The host let her in on the dreadful secret: she was the worst of a season full of America's worst singers. That moment was so crushing to Jamie, and so embarrassing to almost everyone watching, that *Superstar USA* was canceled after one season. There is no nudity so offensive to people as the naked truth.

Jamie did get a check for $50,000 and a recording contract. As you might imagine, thirteen years later the record company still hasn't produced her CD. The joke was on Jamie. It's so easy to believe what isn't so and yet so hard to believe what is. *Superstar USA* only ran for one season, but the ultimate reality show, *Spirituality USA*, runs every day of every year. The judges told Jamie what she wanted to hear. Lots of folks will do the same for us. But the embarrassment and pain that Jamie Foss endured will one day pale in comparison to ours if we allow false flattery to delude us about ourselves. Today, someone or something might smack you in the face with harsh reality. You'll be better for it, if you remember this lesson from Jamie's story:

*Reality denied will always come back to hurt you more than the truth.*

⌘

Faithful are the wounds of a friend;
profuse are the kisses of an enemy.

PROVERBS 27:6, ESV

# The Night Mars Invaded
# New Jersey

୧ல௵ର

There was a time when radio was king. But no one knew just how powerful electronic media was until that October evening in 1938. Some six million listeners were tuned in to the CBS program *The Mercury Theater* when the show was preempted by a frantic news bulletin: "Toronto, Canada. Professor Morse of McGill University has observed a total of three explosions on the planet Mars." Another urgent bulletin followed: "It is reported that at 8:50 p.m. a huge, flaming object, believed to be a meteorite, fell in the neighborhood of Grover's Mill, New Jersey."

The announcer said that CBS had dispatched reporter Carl Phillips to the scene. Twenty seconds later, Phillips was on the air. He described the mass chaos of crowds stampeding over police barricades to see the meteorite. A nationwide radio audience could hear the sounds of sirens, horns, and people shoving and shouting. Soon this bedlam in New Jersey would grip the nation.

Phillips interviewed Princeton scientist Professor Pierson, who declared excitedly that this was not a meteorite but something encased in a metal not found on earth: a cylindrical shape, something extraterrestrial! The reporter interrupted the professor: "Just a minute! Something's happening! Ladies and gentlemen, this is terrific! This end of the thing is beginning to flake off! The top is beginning to rotate like a screw! The thing must be hollow!"

The radio audience could hear the shouts of panicked bystanders. "Look, the darn thing's unscrewing!" "Keep back, there! Keep back, I tell you!" "Maybe there's men in it trying to escape!" Phillips was now screaming about something like a gigantic gray snake coming out of the top. It had tentacles, was as huge as a bear, and glistened like wet leather, with huge black eyes like a serpent. Its mouth was V-shaped, with saliva dripping from rimless lips that seemed to quiver and pulsate.

Reports were coming in rapid fire: spaceships were hovering over the Hudson River; the monster from the space cylinder was incinerating people with heat rays; Martian tripods were obliterating undermanned state police; a report from the governor of New Jersey had declared martial law; and highways were clogged as people fled the aliens.

By now millions of listeners across America were panic stricken. Hysterical people ran into the streets. Phone lines were jammed. Most listeners didn't wait around to hear the final words from *The Mercury Theater*: "You've been listening to the CBS presentation of Orson Wells and *The Mercury*

*Theater* in an original dramatization of *The War of the Worlds* by H. G. Wells."

This innovative use of dramatized fiction became national headlines: RADIO LISTENERS IN PANIC—*New York Times*. RADIO FAKE SCARES NATION—*Chicago Herald*. U.S. TERRORIZED—*San Francisco Chronicle*. The legendary career of Orson Wells was launched, and so was the mega power of mass media. Decades later we are still blitzed by entertainment sold as news, much of it biased or false. That is good enough reason to look for the straight scoop in the Bible. The best thing about the true news is that it is also the good news.

*Truth is powerful, and it will still prevail after every lie has been exposed.*

⸾⸾⸾

All Scripture is inspired by God and is useful
to teach us what is true and to make us realize
what is wrong in our lives. It corrects us when we
are wrong and teaches us to do what is right.

2 TIMOTHY 3:16

# Conceived in Shame,
# Born for Greatness

༄༅

The boy was an outcast, rejected by his father and scorned by his brothers. History remembers his exploits, but the shame of his youth is hidden away in ancient Torah commentaries. It is well known by Jewish rabbis but seldom talked about among Christian scholars.

The boy's father, Yishai, was a member of Judaism's high court, revered as one of the four guardians of the Torah, a man of considerable wealth, and a descendant of Israel's most famous family. He lived on a ranch outside the village of Beit Lechem, south of Jerusalem. His beautiful wife, Nitzevet, gave him seven handsome sons who all grew up to be mighty warriors.

Yishai's life should have been idyllic, except for a single blot on his family name. His grandfather had married a widow from a nearby pagan nation. Any descendants born of that forbidden union were unclean to the tenth generation. Torah law, which Yishai so zealously guarded, said that he and his boys were impure because of his grandfather's illicit marriage.

Over the years, Yishai became obsessed about this stain

on his family name. But he did rejoice in the fact that God had given him seven sons. And he wanted to keep it at seven because that was the Hebrew number for blessing. So he shut his bedroom door to his wife. But Nitzevet was determined to bear another child. After tricking and seducing Yishai, she conceived an eighth son.

Yishai never forgave her. Nor did he accept the child of that deception. He encouraged his other sons to reject their kid brother. The little boy ate at a separate table with his disgraced mother, and his brothers publicly mocked him. Eventually, the despised son was exiled to distant fields to care for the flocks. Shepherds were the outcasts of Jewish society. When Yishai sent his son into the wilderness, it was tantamount to saying that his son was dead to him.

At this point the Bible picked up the boy's story. A disillusioned prophet left a disobedient king to anoint a new man for Israel's throne. God led him to Yishai's farm outside Beit Lechem. A proud dad paraded his seven strapping sons before an impressed prophet. But God whispered, "Beware, Sammy! You're looking at the outward appearances, but I look at the heart." The prophet asked Yishai if he had another son. "Yes," replied the rancher. "But why would you be interested in a shepherd boy?"

Yet the boy had become an eagle eye with a slingshot, killing lions and bears while growing close to God in the lonely wilderness. By now you may have guessed that the boy

Samuel wanted to see was David. We call Yishai "Jesse" and Beit Lechem "Bethlehem." Jesse's grandfather was Boaz, who broke Torah law by marrying a Moabite woman named Ruth. The story of an outcast boy who grew up to be a giant slayer is just one of many that prove this undeniable principle:

*God forges greatness in the furnace of loneliness and affliction.*

---

When you pass through the waters, I will be with you; and through the rivers, they shall not overwhelm you; when you walk through fire you shall not be burned, and the flame shall not consume you.

ISAIAH 43:2, ESV

# When Dogs Routed
# a Tank Division

౿౷౿౩౷౿

S ome of the most colossal blunders have taken place in military history. Many have been devastatingly tragic. Others have been downright silly, like the one that happened in Russia during World War II.

The Soviet Union was reeling under the withering assault of the German blitzkrieg. Within weeks, the Nazi advance had killed four million Russian soldiers. It seemed that Moscow would soon fall. At the cutting edge of Hitler's war machine were the panzer divisions. These sleek tanks raced forward like chariots of fire, leaving a wake of devastation and death. The clumsy and antiquated Russian tanks were no match for the German juggernaut.

These were frantic days in the Kremlin war room. Joseph Stalin demanded quick answers. When the generals and commissars didn't have any, they were sacked or shot. Panic and despair set in. No one knew how to stop the dreaded panzers, until a hotshot young commissar came up with an ingenious idea: dog bombs. His plan was to train dogs to run up under the advancing German tanks with bombs strapped to their backs. The commissar convinced his skeptical superiors that his plan was foolproof.

Hundreds of dogs went through a quick but intensive training program. The day came to put Operation Dog Bomb into action. Russian and German tanks were massing across from each other when a small convoy of Russian trucks pulled up on the field between the two armies. Canines jumped out of the trucks, bombs strapped to their backs. Russian trainers pointed them toward the panzers and blew their whistles.

The Germans looked on in astonishment as packs of dogs came running at them. Suddenly, the dogs stopped and looked both ways in confusion. Then, they turned tail and ran back toward the Soviet battle group and up under *their* tanks. Russian tanks were blowing up right and left. The Russian battle line collapsed in chaos as drivers tried desperately to get away from the pursuing dog bombs.

Surely this was one of the most bizarre battles in the annals of military warfare. Never before or since has a pack of dogs routed a division of tanks! How did this fiasco happen? It seems that the boys in the Kremlin made a slight miscalculation in their preparation. They trained their dogs using *Russian* tanks. The commissar who conceived the idea of dog bombs disappeared from sight after this fiasco.

So many battles have been lost because of bad planning and preparation. The best dog bombs in the world won't work if the dogs are trained on the wrong tanks. Wars are won and lost in the training that takes place before battles begin. The small battles that you face every day are the basic training for bigger wars ahead. Learn your lessons well today so that you will be prepared for what comes tomorrow. Take time to train your children and prepare your family for inevitable battles ahead. You might want to remember this key to success:

*The will to prepare is more important than the will to succeed.*

———— ҩ৯৩ঌ ————

Physical training is good, but training for
godliness is much better, promising benefits
in this life and in the life to come.

1 TIMOTHY 4:8

# The Curse of the Control Freak

⋘⊚⋙

H e was as famous for his craziness as for his paintings that sold for as much as $10,000 in the 1940s. He saw himself as the last of the bohemians: an avant-garde artist in a world of bongos, beards, and beatniks. Hollywood celebrities were drawn to his hillside ranch for wild parties that he hosted in a toga worn over red long underwear. As they wandered his forty-eight-acre junkyard, they marveled at a mishmash of sculptures created out of salvaged wood, rusted bedsprings, and other recycled junk. When the artist stripped naked to show off his body covered with tattoo art, it was the signal for a night of free love, drugs, and alcohol to begin. J. H. Zorthian was a hippie years before the Age of Aquarius.

Most of his Hollywood celebrity guests could not have guessed that there was a time when this crazy Armenian was a conventional mural artist. Back then he lived in a Pasadena neighborhood with an heiress wife and three children. One morning he read a newspaper account about a child who had been run over by a car. Fearing that his own children might suffer a similar fate, he began plotting how he could guarantee his kids' safety in an accident-prone world.

Zorthian's paranoia drove him to sell his home on the streets of Pasadena and purchase a twelve-acre plot in the Altadena Hills at the end of a winding, deserted road. At each turn, the artist posted a sign: "Children at Play." He constructed a fenced-in play area that no automobile could approach. Then he built a house with every safety design possible. Finally, he added a garage. Only one car was allowed to drive up to it, and that was Zorthian's.

After the ranch house was finished, he walked the property in deep thought, considering what other dangers might threaten his children. His last project to tackle was the garage. What if he backed out and accidentally ran over one of the children? Zorthian quickly sketched plans for a protected turnaround, but before the concrete could be poured, heavy rains came. It would have been finished by that weekend if it hadn't rained. Instead, when Zorthian had to back out of the garage on Sunday, his toddler son, Tiran, ran into the path of the car and was killed.

Friends said that J. H. Zorthian never recovered from that tragedy. It caused him to plunge into a free-flowing bohemian lifestyle. Could it be that there's a happy medium between the two extremes of control freak and irresponsible? The more you reflect on Zorthian's story, the more this makes sense:

*Do the best you can. Then relax and leave the results to God.*

———— ✿ ————

We can make our own plans, but the LORD gives the
right answer. People may be pure in their own eyes,
but the LORD examines their motives. Commit your
actions to the LORD, and your plans will succeed.

PROVERBS 16:1-3

# The Compassionate Puritan

Few people have lived or died as well as Jon. He graduated from Yale at the top of his class at age seventeen. While still a teenager, he wrote a paper on metaphysical theology. He then penned a treatise on atomic theory two hundred years before Albert Einstein's work on the topic. Many scholars rate Jon as America's greatest philosopher. His books on metaphysics are masterpieces. No other American has produced more national leaders among his descendants.

Shortly before Jon became the president of Princeton, his scientific curiosity focused on advances in medicine. The science of inoculation was primitive, but when smallpox ravaged colonial America, Jon volunteered to be a human guinea pig. On March 22, 1758, several days after he was inoculated with an experimental vaccination, he died from the disease.

Jon possessed one of the most brilliant minds in American history. His quest for knowledge was insatiable. But if you assume that he took that inoculation for the advancement of medical science, you would be wrong. Most folks would find it hard to believe that he did it because of compassion. History remembers him for his famous sermon "Sinners in the Hands of an Angry God." His portraits reveal a stern Puritan. His call for repentance sparked the revivals that shook colonial America. When he rebuked church leaders for their hypocrisy, he made enemies in high places. After he called out his parishioners for their lukewarm faith, they fired him. History recalls Jonathan Edwards either as a brilliant-but-coldly-rational philosopher or a hellfire-and-brimstone preacher.

Most folks don't know that he spent a year's salary to purchase a black slave and then set her free. He begged Christians everywhere to do the same. Later, he worked among the Mohicans and took up their cause when most colonists despised them. His home was often filled with individuals from various Native tribes, much to the distress of his neighbors. After he was thrown out of his church, he was offered pulpits in prestigious parishes but became a missionary to the impoverished Housatonic tribe of New Jersey. He made even more enemies by going after crooked politicians who tried to steal their land.

When his Native neighbors began dying by the thousands from smallpox, he took that high-risk inoculation in hopes that a cure would be found. He refused to heed friends who argued that his life was too important to risk. The love that compelled him to plead with colonists to flee from hell also drove him to die for those they despised as savages. In his final hours, Edwards's throat was so constricted that he could hardly eat, drink, or breathe. With his final gasping words, he instructed his daughter Lucy to give a portion of his estate to the poor. His physician said that he had never seen a man die with as much calmness and grace as Edwards. Jonathan Edwards not only died well but also lived better by lifting others' burdens. This story of the third president of Princeton University should inspire us with this truth:

*A life well lived is not measured in how many positions we've held, but in how many people we've helped.*

⁓

Pure and genuine religion in the sight
of God the Father means caring for
orphans and widows in their distress.

JAMES 1:27

# Old Woom's Winnie

୧ଡ଼୧ଡ଼ଡ଼ଡ଼

Great things were expected of this firstborn son of a British lord. But the person who was perhaps the greatest influence on his life was not someone with prestige and power; it was his nanny. That woman became the love of this lonely boy's life. As an adult, he often shed tears when he remembered the substitute mother he affectionately called Old Woom. She gave him the nickname Winnie.

When little Winnie wasn't frolicking in the park with Old Woom, he sat alone at his bedroom window watching soldiers drill across the boulevard. He imagined that if he could come back from war as a hero, he might earn his parents' love.

At age seven he began his odyssey through prep schools. He hardly ever saw his folks, except for fleeting moments during holidays. But that didn't keep him from driving himself to make them proud. Not even a speech impediment could stop him once he set his mind on something. This earned him another nickname: pigheaded. He wore that unkind epithet as a badge of honor.

He applied to his nation's leading military college, only to fail the entrance exam three times. Once he got in, he barely made the grades to stay in. As a young officer his career was undistinguished. He came home to run for parliament and was defeated. He headed off to South Africa to fight in the Boer War, but was captured.

When Winnie got back home again, he rose in the ranks of government with the help of family connections. He was finally elected to parliament, but was condemned when he ordered troops to fire on striking miners. During World War I, as first lord of the Admiralty, he committed the greatest blunder of his career when he insisted that British troops seize Gallipoli in Turkey. Over a million soldiers were drawn into that unnecessary battle. Military brass warned Winnie that an advance into the teeth of Turkish artillery was suicidal. But he wouldn't back down. One admiral resigned, calling Winnie pigheaded. Before this debacle ended in defeat, there were 250,000 casualties on both sides. Winnie was sacked.

But with his trademark pigheadedness, he bounced back to become chancellor of the exchequer. Against all advice, he pigheadedly made monetary changes that plunged England into a depression. Again he was fired. When he stood pigheaded against his party's unwillingness to take a stand against Communism and Nazism, Winnie spent his next decade in political isolation. No one would have guessed then that his nation would soon need his pigheadedness. The world remembers Winnie as Prime Minister Winston Churchill, whose refusal to back down saved the world from totalitarianism.

Later, he went on to win the Nobel Prize. In 2002, a BBC poll named him the greatest Briton of all time. When asked the secret to his success, Churchill replied, "Success is the ability to go from failure to failure with no loss of enthusiasm." If you are discouraged today, you might want to recall a line in a speech that pigheaded Winnie gave at Harrow during the worst days of World War II:

*Never give in, never give in, never, never, never, never give in!*

⁂

As for you, be strong and courageous,
for your work will be rewarded.

2 CHRONICLES 15:7

# A Resurrection in the Valley of Death

⋘⊙⊙⋙

When Phil and Stan kissed their wives good-bye, it was for the last time. On September 19, 1968, the Iowa farm boy and his buddy from Australia climbed into the highlands of New Guinea, going where no Westerner had ventured before. But Stan and Phil wanted to bring Jesus to the Yali people. Their vision was audacious. The Yali were headhunters and cannibals, living in the Stone Age. These most-feared of the mountain tribes were called lords of the earth.

Officials warned Phil and Stan that it was sheer suicide to enter the Yali heartland. But the Iowa farm boy and the Australian outbacker were not easily cowed. They had already hacked their way through impassable forests, carved an airfield out of tangled jungle, and built a mission station with their own hands. Stan had fought the Japanese in World War II, survived a ruptured appendix in the jungle, and pulled five Yali arrows from his body in an earlier attack. Phil said, "They can't kill me. I died the day that I gave myself to Jesus."

As the missionaries went over the mountains into the Seng

Valley, they were entering misty shadowlands of witchcraft, revenge killings, and human sacrifices. Distant drums warned that shamans were stirring up their people to destroy these white devils. On September 25, 1968, Stan Dale and Phil Masters went down under a hail of arrows as the Yali swarmed over them. Remembering that these missionaries had talked about a resurrection and fearing that they might come back to haunt them, the Yali hacked their bodies to pieces, ate them, burned their bones, and scattered their ashes into the wind.

When Yali drums carried the news of their death down the valleys of the Snow Mountains, it seemed like a monumental tragedy. They left behind two grieving widows and ten orphaned children. No one was available to finish the translation of the Bible into Yali. Persecution broke out against the handful of Yali believers. Stan Dale's widow went back to Australia, never to return. Phil Masters's widow cried out in despair, "Why, God? What did we do wrong?" For all practical purposes, the vision to reach the Yali was over.

But God had other plans. Three months later, a plane crashed in Yali territory. Everyone on board died except for a nine-year-old boy. A Yali believer found and hid him. When a party of missionaries came to retrieve the boy, Yali leaders were sure that the spirits of Stan and Phil had returned. In fear, they invited the missionaries to share their gospel. Today there are one hundred churches among the Yali. The lords of the earth have come to Christ and are sending their own missionaries to neighboring tribes. Who would have guessed that fierce cannibals would become gospel preachers? When your dreams have been shattered, remember the story of two martyred missionaries and a tribe of headhunters. What's true for them is also true for you:

*It's not over until it's over, and then it's still not over.*

❧

But as for me, I know that my Redeemer lives, and he will stand upon the earth at last. And after my body has decayed, yet in my body I will see God!

JOB 19:25-26

# The Possibilities and Limits of Forgiveness

୧୭୨୬

Eighty-nine of Simon's relatives were murdered in the Nazi Holocaust. As far as he knew, his wife was one of them. He barely escaped death several times while funneled through five SS killing centers. One day while he was still imprisoned, a nurse came looking for a Jew. Any Jew would do. An SS officer had made a deathbed request to talk to one. She led Simon to a man swathed in bandages. He had been burned over most of his body; only his eyes were visible, and he couldn't talk above a whisper.

The Nazi officer ordered Simon to sit on the edge of his bed. He introduced himself as Karl Seidl and said that he was raised a Catholic and had joined the SS against his father's wishes. He then gasped out his final confession as if this Jew were his priest. Seidl spared none of the horrifying details of his years as a Jew killer. He told Simon about the day he found a house where two hundred Jews were hiding and ordered his men to set the building afire. He described the screams of people burning alive. He added that he had personally shot every man, woman, and child who had tried to escape that inferno.

When Seidl finally finished his confession, the room was deathly still. Simon shook with hatred. But SS Officer Seidl desperately wanted absolution. In the mind of this dying Nazi, Simon sat in the place of every Jew he had dehumanized or murdered. Seidl whispered with urgency, "Jew, will you forgive me?" Simon sat for several seconds looking down at the SS officer and then got up and walked away, leaving Karl Seidl to die without absolution.

Two years later, Simon's camp was liberated. He had survived the last year on two hundred calories a day. Miraculously, he was reunited with his wife. He went on to become the world's most celebrated Nazi hunter. Until he died at age ninety-six, he fought anti-Semitism and kept the memory of the Holocaust alive.

Yet Karl Seidl haunted Simon until the day he died. Simon constantly tortured himself with questions about whether he was right in refusing to forgive the SS officer. He remembered a day when his work detail passed a German military cemetery. He saw a sunflower on each grave and wondered if there was one on Seidl's. In 1976, Simon Wiesenthal tried to bury the ghost of Karl Seidl by writing a bestseller entitled *The Sunflower*. In it he discussed the possibilities and limits of forgiveness, asking the questions that haunted him since he walked away from Seidl. In his book, fifty-three distinguished theologians, jurists, human rights activists, Holocaust survivors, and victims of other genocides respond to his questions. They prove one thing: there are no easy answers to forgiveness. Apart from Jesus there are no ultimate answers.

Some two thousand years ago, hardened religious leaders nailed a rabbi from Nazareth to a cross. This Jew responded to those who dehumanized and murdered him, "Father forgive them." Simon Wiesenthal thought that forgiveness was a gift you give someone else and Karl Seidl wasn't worthy. If you think someone hasn't earned your forgiveness, you might want to remember this:

*Forgiveness is the gift that you give yourself.*

⸻ ❧ ⸻

If you forgive those who sin against you,
your heavenly Father will forgive you.

MATTHEW 6:14

# Hugs for the President

❦

Michael felt like an outsider. Maybe it was because he was an adopted kid, or because his Hollywood parents never had time for him. When his folks divorced, he was devastated. After his actor dad married Nancy, things got worse. His new stepmom tolerated no competition for her husband's heart. Eventually, Nancy froze Michael out of the family circle. The lonely boy longed for two things from his father: a hug and the three words "I love you." He got neither.

Michael watched from a distance as his dad went from being president of the Screen Actors Guild, to governor of California, and finally to president of the United States. The only time he was useful to his father was when he was trotted out at some political event to bolster the family image. Michael would stand there with a plastic smile hiding the pain of never cracking the circle of love shared only by Ronnie and Nancy.

Then he turned to Jesus. By grasping how much his heavenly father loved him, he got over his bitterness toward a distant earthly dad. But he still ached for his father to embrace him and say, "I love you." He was devastated when he heard that his dad was in the first stages of Alzheimer's. The clock was ticking. Would Michael ever hear those three words?

One day he saw his dad in a crowded room. His old wounds throbbed again. What would Jesus do? Michael knew the answer. He walked across the room and embraced his startled father. "Dad, I love you." For a moment, the old man was confused. Then he replied softly, "I love you, too." Michael says that every time he saw his father after that, he would hug him and say, "Dad, I love you." After a while, the old president no longer recognized who he was. But he still knew that Michael was the one who always hugged him. Whenever his son came into the room, President Reagan's face would light up as he opened his arms wide for his hug.

Michael saw his dad for the last time a few days before he slipped into a coma. As Michael pulled out of the driveway, his wife tugged at his arm and pointed to the house. His father was standing on the porch, a frail ninety-three-year-old, arms spread wide, waiting for the hug that his son forgot to give him.

At the funeral service for President Reagan, Michael was still shuffled to the outer edges. Nancy never acknowledged his presence. But he had the look of a man at peace. A few days later, he wrote in a news column, "The best gift that my father left me was the knowledge that he had a personal relationship with Jesus, and is waiting for me in heaven."

Maybe you're waiting for a certain someone to show you love. Why don't you take the initiative? Reach out and give a hug. Michael would say amen to this truth:

*Hugs are like boomerangs. Eventually they come back to you.*

———— ✧ ————

He returned home to his father. And while he was still a long way off, his father saw him coming. Filled with love and compassion, he ran to his son, embraced him, and kissed him.

LUKE 15:20

# The Sweet Potato That Destroyed China

⚜

D id you know that the sweet potato destroyed China? If you find this to be an outrageous claim, just ask Charles Mann, the author of the bestselling book *1493*. Better yet, take a trip back to 1492 when Columbus landed in the Bahamas. His great contribution wasn't in discovering America. Voyagers from North Africa may have done that before Christ.

Columbus *did* speed up globalization. Horses, pigs, and smallpox were imported to the New World from Europe. Lemons, oranges, and slaves came from Africa. Spices found their way from Asia. Before Columbus sailed, the French never smoked a cigarette, the Irish hadn't tasted a potato, and the Italians had no tomato sauce. Those commodities existed only in the New World. Columbus didn't discover America, but he opened its treasure trove to the world.

That brings us to the sweet potato, a tasty tuberous root indigenous to South America, and silver, another prevalent natural resource. When a Spanish galleon stumbled upon a Chinese fleet in Manila, traders from China finally saw something they wanted from the West: the New World silver on that Spanish ship. Soon huge fleets of Spanish galleons were transporting tons of Peruvian silver to Manila in exchange for Chinese silk, porcelain, and spices. It was a trade deal made in heaven, until a Chinese merchant saw sweet potatoes on a Spanish ship.

When that trader tasted a baked sweet potato, it was love at first bite. He bought up all the potatoes in the Spanish fleet. Sure enough, the sweet potato became wildly popular in China. Soon the Spanish were bringing bags of these delectable delights along with their silver. The best part of this sweet deal was that the potatoes could be planted in the rocky soil of mountains above fertile rice valleys. But the sweet potato craze led to greedy farmers clearing forests to plant more. Eventually, tropical rains eroded the deforested mountains.

Floods came to the valleys below, wiping out the rice. Famine led to food riots. As emperors of China retreated inside the Forbidden City, warlords rose up to quell the anarchy. Millions were slaughtered. As China's infrastructure collapsed, pestilence stalked the land. A weakened China was taken over by European powers, and it did not recover until fifty years ago—all because of the sweet potato!

Here's a compelling question: what's the "sweet potato" that could destroy America—that thing we crave today that might be remembered as a tragedy four hundred years from now? Could it be our iPhones? We are as crazy about our handheld devices as the Chinese were about their sweet potatoes. Everywhere we go, people ignore each other while staring at a screen, communicating with folks who aren't in the room. Social media multitasking is producing an attention-deficit generation. Never has friendship been so cheaply gained or so easily disposed of as on Facebook. Will future generations talk about the "Apple" that hastened the end of deeply genuine relationships? Today, why don't you put your handheld devices aside and engage in some meaningful face-to-face conversation? Remember this before you pick up today's version of the sweet potato:

*Posting on social media while socializing is unsocial.*

―――― ∽◦◦◦◦ ――――

Let us not neglect our meeting together, as
some people do, but encourage one another.

HEBREWS 10:25

# Searching for Heaven

⚜

John couldn't remember how often he had gone to bed with an empty belly. His single mom barely eked out a living in a tollbooth. When she dragged herself home at night, she had little energy left for her son. Maybe that's why he grew up with a legendary appetite for food, booze, women, and applause.

When his mom died, John dropped out of school and headed for Broadway. When he failed to make it on the stage, he was on to Hollywood. There he landed bit parts in forgettable movies. Along the way, he discovered a knack for slapstick comedy, a flair for music, and the ability to dance with uncommon grace. He channeled those talents into a nightclub act. But he was better known for the orgies in his hotel suite. John was drowning in a sea of booze. His Tinseltown buddies whispered, "Our funny fat friend will never make it."

But John did make it when he landed the lead role in one of television's first sitcoms: *The Life of Riley*. By 1950 he was hosting a variety show that became the highest-rated program on television. Every week, millions tuned in to watch him glide across the stage with America's most beautiful dancers. He created comic characters that are etched in television legend. None is more beloved than bumbling bus driver Ralph Kramden. He parlayed that role into his biggest sitcom, *The Honeymooners*. By now you remember John by his stage name, Jackie. Jackie Gleason starred in twenty-seven movies, recorded sixty-five albums of music, and won almost every award in stage and film before being inducted into television's Hall of Fame.

He made the whole world laugh, but his private life was no laughing matter. He made millions of dollars, only to waste his fortune trying to satisfy his insatiable appetites. Little Johnny grew into fat Jackie, but he could never fill his emptiness. He confessed to friends that there must be something better out there beyond this world. So he became obsessed with parapsychology, UFOs, and extraterrestrials, accumulating the world's largest private library on the paranormal. Jackie even built one of his luxury homes in the shape of a UFO.

Before Gleason died, Mort Sahl of WRC radio asked him, "Jackie, as a man who has seen and done it all, is there anything left that you still want to do?"

The entertainer replied, "I want to see the face of God."

Sahl chuckled uneasily. "Do you mean that you want to go to heaven?"

"I suppose so," replied Gleason. "But mostly, I want to

see God." Then he quietly said, "But I don't know how to get to heaven."

Down deep, everyone wants to see God. Saint Augustine said, "God has created us for himself, and we will be restless until we find our rest in him." Are you hungry today for more? French philosopher Blaise Pascal declared, "Nothing less than heaven will ever satisfy earthlings." Gleason would agree, but he didn't know how to get to heaven. God's Son has an answer for Jackie, and for all of us:

*In Jesus you see the face of God. Through him you get to heaven.*

―――― ∽⊚∾ ――――

Jesus answered, "I am the way and the
truth and the life. No one comes to
the Father except through me."

JOHN 14:6, NIV

# The Miracle on Flight 255

಼ಲ೦ನ

The pilots were in a hurry to take off that Sunday evening. If they didn't clear the runway quickly, they wouldn't beat the noise curfew at their destination in Phoenix. So the McDonnell Douglas rumbled down the runway despite the fact that the pilots hadn't gone through their taxi checklist. Had they done so, they might have discovered that they didn't have electrical power to the aircraft takeoff system. They also would have known that the slats and flaps of their airliner were not extended enough.

As flight 255 lifted off the Detroit runway, the jet began to rock laterally. It struck a light pole, severing eighteen feet off its left wing and igniting stored fuel. The right wing was seared off as it ripped through a car rental building. Rolling crazily out of control, the jetliner careened through traffic and slammed into an overpass on Interstate 94. It then exploded into a fireball, scattering its charred remains across several miles.

It was one of the worst tragedies in airline history. One hundred fifty-four passengers and crew members perished, as well as two motorists on the highway. Only a handful of airline crashes have killed more children and wiped out more entire families than flight 255.

The Detroit medical examiner was one of the first people on the scene. He shook his head and declared that it was impossible that anyone could have survived. As rescuers combed through the burned corpses in the eerie darkness, it seemed that his initial assessment was correct.

Then someone heard a child's faint whimper. Miraculously, four-year-old Cecelia Cichan was huddled under the charred body of her mother, next to the remains of her father and brother. The little girl was critically injured and bearing scars that she will carry for the rest of her life, but she was alive!

After the rescuers pulled the child from the wreckage, the medical examiner closely studied the position of the bodies. He concluded that in the terrifying seconds prior to impact, somehow Cecelia's mother managed to wrap herself around her little girl. Her body not only cushioned the impact but also took the full fury of the fireball that roared through the disintegrating cabin.

Cecelia's mother's act of love gives us a glimpse of what Jesus did on the cross. Our world careens out of control like Northwest flight 255. Like those reckless pilots, humankind has repeatedly violated the safety rules laid out by our loving Creator. As a result, the flames of destruction race toward us. But Jesus wraps himself around God's children. On the cross, he takes the full fireball of hell. Like little Cecelia, we emerge from life's wreckage wounded and scarred. But we have a second chance at eternal life because Jesus shielded us from destruction.

Thirty years later, Cecelia is a wife and mom herself. Every day she thanks God for a mother who was willing to wrap herself around her daughter. Have you allowed Jesus to wrap himself around you? If he has, are you content to remain in the only shelter that will stand up to the firestorms of life?

*If Jesus is your refuge, you no longer have to search for other shelter.*

∽∾∾

[Jesus said,] "How often I have longed
to gather your children together, as a hen
gathers her chicks under her wings."

MATTHEW 23:37, NIV

# The Man Who Changed Washington

⚜

The Reverend Peter Miller made plenty of enemies taking on unpopular causes. But none upset the townsfolk of Ephrata in Lancaster County more than when he left the pulpit of the Reformed church to join a commune of mystics. Michael Widman, who took over Miller's pulpit, especially hated the former pastor. In every sermon, the new preacher castigated Miller as a heretic. Whenever Miller came into town, Widman would scream insults at him. But Peter always responded to his tormentor with a smile, saying, "God loves you, as do I."

Later, Widman quit his pulpit and purchased the town's tavern. When the American Revolution began, he formed a militia. But pacifist Peter Miller refused to take up arms against the British. Widman mocked him as a coward. But the fact that Miller declined to join the militia didn't mean that he wasn't a patriot. In fact, he was one of George Washington's most trusted spies.

One night, when British officers visited his tavern, Widman cursed them and their General Howe. When the redcoats drew swords and pistols, he jumped out the window. He spent days in hiding while they combed the countryside looking for him. Fearing for his life, he turned himself in to the British and offered to spy for them. The loudmouth who bullied Peter Miller for not bearing arms against the English was now spilling his guts to them. General Howe was so disgusted by Widman's cowardice that he had him thrown out onto the streets.

The disgraced tavern owner returned to Ephrata under the cover of dark. When his wife found out what he had done, she told everyone. You might think that Peter Miller rejoiced that his tormentor had been exposed as a fraud. Instead, when word came that his old enemy had been sentenced to hang for treason, Miller walked seventy miles to Valley Forge to plead for Widman's life. General Washington responded, "I'm sorry, Peter, but I cannot release your friend Michael." The reverend replied, "My friend? Sir, he is my worst enemy!" Washington responded, "If you would walk all this way to beg a pardon for your worst enemy, that makes a difference. I will release him to you."

The pacifist took the coward by the arm and led him home. Widman would pay a terrible price for his treason. He lost his tavern, was despised by his wife, and became an outcast. Peter Miller was the only one who refused to abandon him. Maybe that's why a postscript to this story is so touching. Not long after Widman's escape from the gallows, the notorious traitor Joseph Bettys had a rope around his neck when his family arrived to plead for his life. Washington was so touched that he personally removed the noose from Bettys. He then issued a directive to his army to show compassion toward captured enemies. Later, he issued more pardons than any president in US history. Is it possible that the father of our country was changed the day Peter Miller pleaded for the life of his worst enemy? Maybe we can change our world by remembering this:

*We will defeat our enemies when we make them our friends.*

⟡

You have heard that it was said, "Love
your neighbor and hate your enemy."
But I tell you, love your enemies and
pray for those who persecute you."

MATTHEW 5:43-44, NIV

# The Goose from Goose Town

಄ಀ಄

He was nicknamed the Goose. Maybe it was because he hailed from Goose Town. Perhaps it was his fiery temper. When he flew into a rage, he looked like an attacking goose. Yet this peasant dreamed of becoming a gentleman. A single question haunted him: how does a goose become a swan? When he decided that religion was the answer, he became a priest. His sermons packed the Bethlehem Church of Prague, and his bishop bragged that he was the best preacher in Europe. Still Goose felt like he couldn't do enough to be God's swan.

Everything changed when he read a book by the English Reformer John Wycliffe, who claimed that regular folk could get to heaven through faith in Christ's work alone. In Wycliffe's radical theology, Goose found his answer to being transformed into heaven's swan: if his goodness wasn't enough, there was more than enough goodness from heaven!

When he began to preach Wycliffe's message, the Goose ignited a firestorm that got him labeled an archenemy of the faith. He was arrested and imprisoned in the archbishop's palace. In November of 1414 the Vatican convened a council at Constance to deal with him. There, he was jailed in a Dominican monastery, where raw human sewage from the latrines rained down on him. Though he was suffering from pneumonia, he was dragged day after day to face the full fury of a church gone mad. During a break in his trial, he was moved to a castle dungeon where he was shackled for several more months. When the council reconvened, he was carted off to a Franciscan priory, where inquisitors tortured him in a last-ditch effort to break his resolve. Goose still refused to recant.

Finally, he was excommunicated and condemned to the stake. As he neared the place of execution, someone used his nickname as a taunt: "Your goose is cooked!" Wood and straw were piled up to his neck, and a fire was set ablaze with Wycliffe's books as kindling. The Goose died singing an old, traditional hymn. Later, his tormentors scattered his ashes in the Rhine River. But that didn't stop Czech patriots from rising up with the shout, "Remember the Goose!" With that cry of freedom, they threw off the shackles of the medieval church to establish a free nation.

There is an inspiring epilogue to Goose's story. As he was chained to his stake, he uttered a prophecy: "You may cook a goose today, but a hundred years from now a man will rise up whose call for reform cannot be suppressed." Exactly 103 years to the month after Goose was arrested, Martin Luther nailed his ninety-five theses to a door in Wittenberg, igniting a reformation that could not be suppressed. On that day a cooked goose rose from his ashes and soared like a swan. Some six hundred years later the world remembers Goose by his given name, John Huss. If you long to see changes in your life, start with a secret that John Wycliffe gave to the Goose:

*When your goodness isn't good enough, there is a goodness from heaven more than good enough.*

⎯⎯ ⌘ ⎯⎯

He said to me, "My grace is sufficient for you,
for my power is made perfect in weakness."
Therefore I will boast all the more gladly about my
weaknesses, so that Christ's power may rest on me.

2 CORINTHIANS 12:9, NIV

# Letters from Lizzie

తుల

Lizzie allowed herself to be defined by everyone else. Her readers declared her a prodigy when she published four books of poetry before she was twelve years old. By the time she was seventeen, she was the toast of the literary world. Yet her adoring public never saw her. Doctors had declared her an invalid for life after a spinal injury. Years later, her readers would have been shocked to know that England's greatest female poet was a thirty-nine-year-old recluse who seldom left her bedroom. But a struggling poet had fallen in love with her poetry. The two carried on a romance through some of the most passionate love letters ever written.

When he showed up to visit Lizzie, her Victorian parents were outraged. Her father informed the young man that he wasn't good enough and showed him the door. But Lizzie escaped her father's cold house and ran off to Italy with her young poet. In that sunny climate she regained her health and wrote her best poetry. But her angry parents gave her a new definition: ungrateful daughter.

Lizzie wrote them every week for the next decade, begging their forgiveness. After sending more than five hundred unanswered letters, she received a package from her father. She excitedly ripped it open and then burst into tears. In that parcel were all the letters that Lizzie had sent every week for ten years. None had been opened. Her poet husband tried to console his brokenhearted wife, but she never recovered from her parents' final rejection.

What parent wouldn't be thrilled to receive from their children the sort of letters written by Elizabeth Barrett with the encouragement of her poet husband, Robert Browning? We can't help but feel outrage at her parents and sorrow for Lizzie's heartbreak. But the real tragedy for Elizabeth Barrett was in how she allowed others to define her. Doctors declared her an invalid, so she stayed in bed. Her family decided what was best for her health, so she became a recluse. It was only when her authoritarian father declared that her poet lover wasn't good enough that Lizzie finally found the courage to escape a world defined by others. Yet having once escaped their narrow boundaries, Lizzie would spend the rest of her days in a world of sadness that she allowed her unforgiving parents to create for her.

Lizzie's story whispers a warning to all of us: we cannot allow others to define who we are. We live in a fallen world of flawed sinners. By definition the assessment of others, whether positive or negative, is faulty at best and downright wrong at worst. Only the God who created and is recreating us in his image has the right to define who we are. So start living by this credo:

*Strong people let God define them. Weak people let others define them.*

───── ༄ ─────

See what great love the Father has lavished on
us, that we should be called children of God!
And that is what we are! The reason the world
does not know us is that it did not know him. . . .
What we will be has not yet been made known.
But we know that when Christ appears, we
shall be like him, for we shall see him as he is.

1 JOHN 3:1-2, NIV

# The Ship That God Couldn't Sink

ᴄᴏᴏᴏᴅ

In the spring of 1912 the world stood in awe. A colossus was setting out on her maiden voyage. The pride of the White Star Line was a marvel of modern engineering. At 882 feet long, she was the largest ocean liner ever built. The docks were packed with Brits who came to watch this floating palace steam out to sea.

With Victorian smugness, the press proclaimed that the impossible had been done with the building of this unsinkable ship. It was the apex of Darwinian evolution. The captain boasted, "Even God himself cannot sink the *Titanic*." Man was not only master of the seas; he was greater than God himself!

Some forty-eight hours later, on a clear April night, the ship *Titanic* grazed the side of an iceberg. It was so slight that most passengers hardly felt it. Yet it tore a three-hundred-foot-long gash in the hull. Within three hours the "unsinkable" *Titanic* sank four hundred miles south of Newfoundland, taking 1,500 people down to a watery grave.

It was a voyage doomed by pride. The *Titanic* exuded the

class system of the late nineteenth century. On its luxurious top deck were opulent staterooms reserved for society's elite like Vanderbilt, Astor, and Gould. Below them were the second-class decks for the more moderately well-off bourgeois. In the *Titanic*'s bowels were third-class decks crammed with poor immigrants and ship's workers.

The White Star Line was so paranoid about keeping the social classes separate that the doors between the decks were locked and chained. As a result, hundreds of passengers were trapped below. Hundreds more died needlessly because arrogant shipbuilders were cocksure that they had built a megaship that even God couldn't sink. As a result, they didn't think it necessary to provide enough lifeboats.

When news of the tragedy reached England, frantic relatives rushed to the Liverpool offices of the White Star Line to discover if their loved ones had survived. Outside the office was a single wooden board. On it were listed two columns of names. At the top of one was the word "SAVED." Topping the other was the word "LOST." No one was listed according to status or wealth. Astor, Vanderbilt, and Gould were listed among immigrants, waiters, and maids.

Only one thing mattered to those who rushed to the White Star offices to learn their loved ones' fates: were they lost or saved? It would do us all good to stand there at the offices of the White Star Line with those folks on a cool April morning in 1912. We should realize that the SS *Earth* is like an ocean liner plowing through cosmic seas. She is divided into social classes: winners and losers, haves and have-nots, celebrities and nobodies. So many of us are striving to move up to a higher deck. But there's an iceberg out there. Sooner than we think, a sinkable SS *Earth* will collide with the end of time. Only one thing will matter on that day: Are you saved or lost? Before we hit that iceberg, we need to grab hold of this:

***Jesus Christ is not one of many ways to heaven. He is the only way.***

⁓

There is salvation in no one else! God
has given no other name under heaven
by which we must be saved.

ACTS 4:12

# George Washington's Liar

꿍꿍

No one imagined that Ben would become the stuff of legend. But when this shopkeeper heard that British troops had massacred citizens in Boston, something inside him exploded. He cried out in a town meeting, "Good God, are the Americans all asleep and tamely giving up their glorious liberties?" When revolution broke out, he organized a militia and led it down the road to join the fight in Boston.

Then he came up with an audacious idea. If he took Fort Ticonderoga in nearby New York, he could capture enough cannons to blast the British out of Boston. After a forced march, Ben's little militia caught the redcoats napping and took the fort. His feat galvanized a revolution badly in need of a victory. After he was promoted to colonel, he marched his men across Maine's rugged wilderness in freezing November and attacked Quebec with only about a thousand men. A musket ball tore through his leg, leaving him a cripple. But he limped home a hero. After that, he led his men to a string of stunning victories.

Jealous superiors grudgingly promoted him to brigadier general. He had hoped for more. Maybe that's when bitterness took root. Finally, George Washington made him a major general. He alone understood what military experts now affirm: Ben was the greatest general on either side in this war. Ben's star reached its zenith at the Battle of Saratoga. The colonials were in retreat when Ben wheeled his horse around and charged into British cannon fire. His horse was shot out from under him, and he was badly wounded. But his courage rallied the Americans, and victory was snatched from defeat.

Yet there was a dark side to Washington's favorite general. The public hero was a private thief who regularly diverted war funds into his personal accounts. As military governor of Philadelphia, his embezzlement became so egregious that he was court-martialed. Ben appealed to Washington, "Having become a cripple in service to my country, I little expected such ungrateful returns." In a move that still confounds historians, Washington countermanded the court-martial and gave Ben command of the most critical fortress in America's defense system.

Within days, an embittered Ben cut a secret deal to turn the fort over to the enemy in exchange for £20,000 and a commission as a general in the British army. You remember Ben by his birth name, Benedict. The fort he betrayed was West Point. Had the war ended at Saratoga, Benedict Arnold would be celebrated as a hero. Instead, his very name is synonymous with treachery.

It is a baffling mystery: How could George Washington, a man famous for never telling a lie, be so completely conned by one of history's greatest liars? Today, you will be assaulted by a blitzkrieg of lies, cleverly disguised by the enemy of our souls. Maybe the answer to why George Washington and all of us are so easily conned is found in a statement by the Dutch humanist Erasmus:

*Our minds are so formed that we are far more susceptible to falsehood than truth.*

——— ✃ ———

Dear friends, do not believe every spirit, but test the spirits to see whether they are from God, because many false prophets have gone out into the world.

1 JOHN 4:1, NIV

# Two Minutes That Changed History

e◈ఔచౢ

He slumped over his desk in weariness. His face looked like the cracked leather of his old chair. Some fifty-one thousand boys had been slaughtered on a Pennsylvania battlefield, and he was expected to say a few words in memorial to the fallen. So he labored deep into the night for something better than pious platitudes from a worn-out politician.

But inspiration didn't come easily. His screaming wife was suffering one of those migraine headaches that had turned their loveless marriage into a nightmare. He laid his pen aside and escaped next door with his half-written speech. His neighbor agreed that it was a poor start. Overwhelmed with melancholy, he fell into his lonely bed for another sleepless night.

Early the next morning, he caught his train for a grueling journey to the battlefield. He again tried to finish his speech, but it hardly mattered anyway. The main eulogy was to be delivered by Edward Everett, the golden-tongued orator from Massachusetts. The lonely man on the train was invited as an afterthought to give a few closing remarks. The invitation bluntly stated that he should speak a couple of minutes at most. No one ever wanted to follow an Edward Everett speech. And he felt that the words he had scratched out were unworthy of this hallowed occasion.

At ten o'clock in the morning on November 19, the tired man rode across the battlefield being dedicated to the fifty-one thousand slaughtered boys. Most of their corpses still lay in hastily dug graves. More than ten thousand spectators had jam-packed the fields around the grandstand, waiting for Everett's speech. America's greatest orator didn't disappoint. His address lasted more than two hours, making it the longest speech in US history. When he finished, the applause was thunderous.

Then the next speaker, who was an afterthought, got up to deliver his closing remarks. They lasted two minutes, containing only 272 words. When he finished, he was greeted with deathly silence. His heart sank. Slumping next to his friend Ward Lamon, he whispered, "My talk went sour." To the day he died, the man would rank this as his worst speech. To his surprise, applause began to ripple across the fields, growing into a deafening ovation. *Harper's Weekly* later reported, "It was the perfect piece of American eloquence." Newspapers hailed it as the greatest speech in history. Edward Everett said that in just two minutes Abraham Lincoln had captured the heart of Gettysburg better than his two-and-a-half-hour speech.

There was a time when every schoolchild memorized these remarks by a speaker who was invited as an afterthought only because he was the president. That Gettysburg Address gives a simple message: we cannot allow the dead to have died in vain. It is always up to the living to continue the work of those who died to give us a heritage. You might want to find a copy of those two minutes delivered by Abraham Lincoln at Gettysburg. Reading it may inspire you to remember this:

*It is for the living to complete the unfinished work of the dead.*

---

All these people earned a good reputation
because of their faith, yet none of them received
all that God had promised. For God had
something better in mind for us, so that they
would not reach perfection without us.

HEBREWS 11:39-40

# The Monster from Milwaukee

The most horrifying thing about Jeffrey wasn't what came out in his sensational trial. For most folks, it's what happened to him later on in prison. Jeffrey was a serial killer before mass murders became commonplace news in America. Today we hardly get time to digest one act of terror before we are confronted with another. But in the early 1990s, Jeffrey's horror story captivated the nation. Eleven corpses had been found in his apartment. Before the investigation ended, it was discovered that he had murdered and dismembered at least seventeen young men. But the grisly discovery that horrified America was the fact that this sadistic killer also cannibalized his victims.

Search the Internet, and you will find pictures of the monster from Milwaukee sitting in the courtroom during his trial. He sits serenely with steely eyes and an impassive face. There are no signs of remorse or hints of regret. It's no wonder that the world cheered when he was sentenced to life without parole. Even that seemed like too little justice. How could the state ever exact enough retribution for those that this monster had lured into his chamber of horrors?

But this is what folks still find most disturbing: Jeffrey Dahmer became a born-again Christian in prison. He publicly repented for his despicable deeds. After he was baptized, he sent letters of apology to his victims' families. Most people were skeptical, dismissing his newfound faith as a jailhouse conversion. Others were outraged, arguing that God would never forgive such a monster.

Then Jeffrey did the craziest thing in his crazy life. He asked to be released from solitary confinement. Prison officials told him that he was signing his own death warrant. But the born-again serial killer wanted to share his faith. So he was transferred to the general prison population. The chaplain was so impressed by Jeffrey's spiritual growth that he made him his assistant. The monster from Milwaukee was now reading the Scriptures and serving Communion.

At the same time, fellow prisoners were plotting to kill him. When an inmate slashed his throat, he miraculously survived. His parents begged him to return to solitary confinement. Jeffrey responded that prison was his mission field. A few days later, he was beaten to death in a prison restroom. When the news of his death was broadcast on November 28, 1994, the nation cheered. It was Thanksgiving day all over again.

Yet there was one fly in the ointment of justice. The prison chaplain told skeptical reporters that Jeffrey Dahmer was truly saved and in heaven. That claim sparked a national debate: Aren't there some sins and sinners so heinous that they are beyond God's grace? Maybe these questions are more relevant: are some sins in your life beyond God's grace? Can others hurt you so badly that they are beyond your forgiveness? Jeffrey's story is disturbing, but it drives us to consider something Corrie ten Boom said when she was faced with forgiving those who abused and killed her sister in a Nazi concentration camp:

*No pit is so deep that God is not deeper still.*

———— ∽◎◎∾ ————

I could ask the darkness to hide me and the
light around me to become night—but even
in darkness, I cannot hide from you.

PSALM 139:11-12

# The Broken Harpsichord

The old composer was in the twilight of life. He was only fifty-seven years of age, but he seemed so much older. Always misshapen in appearance, he now looked like a hunchbacked gnome. A tempestuous past had finally worn his soul down to a nub. He had overcome so much. His mother tried to abort him, his grandfather rejected him, and his father almost destroyed him. Though he was a musical prodigy, his dyslexia made it difficult for him to read or write. He was ugly in appearance, melancholy in temperament, and painfully shy. Rejected by every woman he ever loved, he would live out his life in loneliness.

Almost all of his fees went to support a family left destitute by his drunken father. Yet poverty didn't impede productivity. He drove himself with perfectionistic frenzy to earn the approval he craved. Some two hundred years later, his soaring symphonies still leave us breathless. They also reveal the inner rage that drove him to write such gloriously tempestuous scores.

Just as he experienced success, he contracted an incurable disability. He drove himself to compose as many works as possible in the short time left. As his disability increased, so did his miraculous output. Yet his obsessive-compulsive personality, fueled by emotional turmoil, ruined almost all his friendships. Critics complained that his symphonies were strange, overtly extravagant, and even risqué. He would utter these cynical words on his deathbed: "Plaudite, amici, comoedia finite est." (Applaud friends, the comedy is over.)

In his final days, he spent long evenings playing a broken-down harpsichord that had been sold cheaply at auction. Its finish was faded; keys were missing. And it was hopelessly out of tune. Yet tears of joy flowed down the composer's face when he played that wreck of a harpsichord. Those watching said that the malformed body became serenely beautiful. Maybe he had finally begun to relax after fifty-seven years of frantic turbulence.

His servants would look at each other with sly grins. You would think that old Ludwig van Beethoven was hearing a symphony from heaven instead of the sour notes on a broken instrument. And maybe he was! As you may know, the disability that should have ruined his career was the loss of his hearing. It was a miracle that he could have written symphonies for the ages when he was going deaf. Now he existed in a world of total silence. But he was hearing the music that the harpsichord *should* make, not the sour notes it *did* make.

Do you ever feel like Beethoven's wreck of a harpsichord—faded and peeling, with your best days behind you? Are you a few ivories short of a full keyboard? Remember this, dear friend: God has purchased you with the priceless sacrifice of his only begotten Son. He's not deaf like Beethoven. He hears all your sour notes. But he chooses to enjoy your best ones and loves you all the more for those that aren't so good. The story of Beethoven's harpsichord gives this hope:

*God plays his most beautiful symphonies on broken instruments.*

———— ✧ ————

Don't be afraid, for I am with you. Don't be discouraged, for I am your God. I will strengthen you and help you. I will hold you up with my victorious right hand.

ISAIAH 41:10

# The Price We Pay for Love

⸎

Clive wrote about faraway places he never visited. He created magical worlds seen through children's eyes though he was a middle-aged college professor. He wrote a bestselling book on love even though he had never experienced romance. Later he authored a book on the problem of pain in spite of the fact that he was living a comfortable life. When his nation's capital was being bombed into rubble, he lifted the spirits of his countrymen with rousing radio talks. Yet he lived far from the bombs in a peaceful university town.

In short, Clive was the world's foremost expert on things he had never experienced. The biggest excitement in his life was sitting at the same table in the same pub on the same evening every week with the same cronies, creating adventures that they would never experience in places they would never visit. Beyond that, he was a slightly dumpy professor who shared a cluttered cottage with his bachelor brother.

Then Clive's life was turned upside down by a visiting author from America. Joy would give him the greatest happiness in his life, only to leave him to cope with unbearable grief.

The two were polar opposites. She was a recent divorcée while he was a confirmed bachelor. Where he was stodgy, she was flamboyant. He was boringly conventional. She loved to flout tradition. He was a staunch Anglican. She jumped impulsively from Judaism to communism to evangelicalism. Yet in spite of their stark differences, Joy and Clive formed a deep friendship that eventually blossomed into love.

Just when the fifty-eight-year-old bachelor ratcheted up his courage to propose, she discovered that she had terminal bone cancer. He wanted to call off the wedding, insisting that losing a wife would be too painful. Joy responded, "The extent to which we love each other now is the extent to which you will feel pain after I'm gone. That's the deal."

It took Clive several days to realize that having Joy now was worth the pain later. On March 21, 1957, they were married in her hospital room. The next few years were deliriously happy. Then she died of cancer, plunging him into suicidal despair that almost destroyed his faith. He recovered enough to write *A Grief Observed*. A haunting line leaps off one of its pages: "I not only live each endless day in grief, but live each day thinking about living each day in grief."

Three years after cancer stole his beloved Joy, he collapsed in his bedroom and died. The world hardly noticed the passing of this author of the beloved Chronicles of Narnia because a young American president was assassinated in Dallas on the same day. But fifty-four years later, C. S. Lewis is remembered as a towering giant who changed the landscape of literature. Maybe you're facing the loss of someone or something very special. Perhaps you are grieving for a loss already suffered. You might take some solace in "the deal" offered by Joy Davidman to her fearful English bachelor:

*The pain of your loss is living proof of the joy you possessed.*

⁕

May the God of hope fill you with all joy and peace
as you trust in him, so that you may overflow
with hope by the power of the Holy Spirit.

ROMANS 15:13, NIV

# Kissing the Beggar's Lips

೮ಾಂ

He was christened Giovanni, the Italian name for John. His mother named him after John the Baptist in hopes that he would be devoted to Jesus. But Giovanni was hardly devout. As the son of a wealthy cloth merchant, the boy was a spoiled rich kid. Though his father hoped he would take over the family business, Giovanni frittered away his days listening to troubadours in the marketplace. At night he played the fop, prancing from one debauchery to another. He wasted his father's money on prostitutes and his energy in street brawls. Yet he existed in disillusionment and despair.

One day a beggar in the marketplace asked Giovanni for a handout. His rich young friends shoved the panhandler aside. But Giovanni remembered a line he heard at Sunday Mass: "When you feed the hungry, you minister to Christ." He grabbed hold of the beggar, gave him everything in his pockets, and kissed him full on his lips.

That evening he informed his family that he wanted to give everything away to the poor. His enraged father forced Giovanni to enlist in the army, and he was sent off to war. After he was captured, he said that Christ visited him in his prison. When he returned home, he no longer wanted to party with his friends. They jokingly asked if he was planning to marry and settle down. He replied, "Yes, I shall soon wed Lady Poverty." He moved into a charity hospital where he fed and bathed the most repulsive of the sick. On winter nights he climbed into bed with lepers, wrapping them in his arms to keep them warm.

By day, this son of wealth sat on the steps of the cathedral begging for money to feed the poor. When his father's cardinal friend, the confessor to Pope Innocent, came up the steps, he begged for permission to start a new order to minister to the poor. With the pope's blessing, he gathered disciples who gave away all their possessions to follow Jesus. They crisscrossed Europe, ministering to the poor, comforting the sick, and evangelizing the forgotten. Giovanni was the only missionary that the caliph ever allowed to preach in North Africa. This supreme leader of Islam said, "He is the rarest of all Christians who truly lives out his faith."

While still in his early forties, Giovanni caught a fatal disease from a sick wretch that he held in his arms. In October of 1226 he fell prostrate on the cold ground and whispered, "Welcome, Sister Death." Then he gasped his final words to his brothers: "I have done my part. May Jesus teach you to do yours." You remember Giovanni di Bernardone by the name his father later gave him: Francesco. History memorializes him as St. Francis of Assisi. His last words challenge each of us. Have we done our part? If you don't know what your part is, ask Jesus. If you already know but find it impossible to accomplish, Jesus stands ready to give you what St. Francis said makes it possible:

*To give largely, liberally, and cheerfully requires a new heart.*

⸻ ♋ ⸻

I will give you a new heart and put a new
spirit in you; I will remove from you your
heart of stone and give you a heart of flesh.

EZEKIEL 36:26, NIV

# A Lifeline from the Asylum

☙☙☙

H e was one of those wretched souls locked away in an insane asylum in the 1800s. He insisted that he wasn't crazy. But the science of psychology was still in its infancy. In those days, asylums were more like prisons. The misdiagnosed, the mildly eccentric, and the "raving lunatics" were all thrown in together. Methods for treating the mentally ill were cruel and primitive. If you weren't mentally unstable when they committed you, you were certain to lose your sanity afterward.

When he finally died, the workers who came to clean up his cell discovered a poem scribbled on the wall next to his bed. The doctors were perplexed. How could a lunatic articulate such beauty? Actually, they weren't his words. Before they locked him away in the asylum, he had memorized lines written by a Jewish rabbi some nine hundred years earlier. He must have scratched them on the wall as a lifeline of hope when he was drowning in a rising sea of insanity. Years later, a discouraged evangelist turned these lines into the last stanza of a famous hymn:

*Could we with ink the ocean fill*
  *And were the skies of parchment made,*
*Were every stalk on earth a quill*
  *And every man a scribe by trade,*
*To write the love of God above*
  *Would drain the ocean dry.*
*Nor could the scroll contain the whole*
  *Though stretched from sky to sky.*

*O love of God, how rich and pure!*
  *How measureless and strong!*
*It shall forevermore endure*
  *The saints' and angels' song.*

Maybe you have joined the countless millions who have sung the hymn "The Love of God." You probably didn't know that it was based on the words of a medieval rabbi who was defending a group of Jews from anti-Semitic attacks or that it was later scribbled on the wall of an insane asylum. There's something poignant about this poor soul clinging to those words as the light of his soul slowly dimmed and then went out. Were these words his last touch with sanity?

How that story was passed on is a story in itself. A worker who cleaned the room wrote them in pencil on a scrap of paper. That paper passed through many hands over several years. A discouraged evangelist found it lying on an apple crate in the corner of a room and turned its words into the third verse of his hymn.

These words run like a thread of hope through so many stories: a rabbi running for his life; an inmate fighting to keep his sanity; an evangelist trying to find hope; and countless millions who have been inspired by a hymn. Isn't the sustaining power of a story amazing? Now the words have found their way to you. Maybe you should scribble them on your wall too.

*Hope is the raw material from which faith builds the house.*

෴

Hope does not put us to shame, because God's love has been poured out into our hearts through the Holy Spirit, who has been given to us.

ROMANS 5:5, NIV

# Little Herbie Steals a Quarter

❧

Herbie was the sweetest little boy in the Maywood neighborhood of Indianapolis. He might have grown up to be an angel if his doting mother hadn't died when he was four years old. Instead, his harsh father bullied him at home, turning him into a playground bully at school.

By the time he was a sixth grader, he was a back-alley brawler and petty thief. He dropped out after middle school and became a drifter. At age twenty he was arrested for stealing a car and joined the navy to avoid prosecution. But he soon deserted and was dishonorably discharged. He got married, but his violent temper killed the romance, and the marriage ended in a bitter divorce. After he and a buddy held up a grocery store, he was sentenced to twenty years for armed robbery. When he entered the Indiana State Prison, he snarled, "I will be the meanest SOB you ever saw when I get out of here!"

When he was paroled eight years later, his gang became the most prolific bank robbers in US history. His daring jailbreaks became the stuff of tabloid legend. He bragged to a reporter, "All my life I wanted to be a bank robber, carry a gun, and wear a mask. Now that it's happened, I guess I'm about the best bank robber they ever had. And I sure am happy."

The public adored him as something of a modern-day Robin Hood, but Herbie was a vicious psychopath who hobnobbed with notorious gangsters like "Pretty Boy" Floyd and "Baby Face" Nelson. J. Edgar Hoover declared him Public Enemy Number One and launched the biggest manhunt in US history to bring him to justice.

Maybe you remember Herbie by his full name: John Herbert Dillinger. Mary Dillinger's little angel had grown up to be the meanest man you ever saw. Not long before he was shot down in an FBI ambush, John Dillinger confided to a friend, "I can trace my life of crime back to when I was nine years old. I stole a quarter from my old man's wallet. I was scared that he would find out and give me a beating, but I got away with it. After that, stealing became easy."

Little Herbie stole a quarter. It didn't seem like a big deal at the time. But it led to a lifetime of choices that created John Dillinger, Public Enemy Number One. No choice is insignificant. Your decisions are the hinges on which your destiny hangs. French philosopher Albert Camus wrote, "Life is the sum of all your choices." John Dillinger was no philosopher, but he would probably agree with Camus.

You will make thousands of choices today. A few may be carefully weighed, but most will be impulsive or unconscious. The vast majority probably won't warrant a second thought. But none will be unimportant. So do yourself a favor. Reflect long and hard on the story of a little boy who stole a quarter. Your decisions today may not lead to such high drama, but this much is true for each of us:

*Monumental consequences are shaped by momentary choices.*

---

Trust in the LORD with all your heart and
do not lean on your own understanding.
In all your ways acknowledge Him, and
He will make your paths straight.

PROVERBS 3:5-6, NASB

# The Cinderella Man

⌒⊙⌒

Jimmy had been a contender. Now he was a club fighter, slugging it out for a few bucks and beers. When he broke his right hand, he was forced to quit the ring. After he lost his job as a day laborer, he had to take handouts to feed his family. The former heavyweight contender was now a welfare recipient.

Yet through a series of events that could only have been dreamed up by a Hollywood scriptwriter, Jimmy found himself in a Long Island stadium fighting Max Baer, the undisputed heavyweight champion of the world. Baer took sadistic delight in knocking his opponents senseless. Two fights earlier, he had beaten a challenger to death in the ring. In his last fight, he had battered another into permanent brain damage. Baer's managers had booked the fight with Jimmy thinking that the washed-up bum from Hoboken would be an easy walkover.

Jimmy desperately needed the money. He went into that fight as a staggering twenty-to-one underdog. Yet on June 13, 1935, Jim Braddock scored the greatest upset in sports history by beating Max Baer. He has been dubbed the

Cinderella Man for his magical feat. When asked how he overcame such overwhelming odds, Braddock replied, "No matter how many times I'm knocked down, I always get up and fight one more round."

His upset victory gave hope to a nation mired in the Great Depression. In 1935, one out of every three men in America was standing in a soup line. Less than 25 percent of those who did have a job were earning an adequate wage. The suicide rate was at an all-time high. But when Jimmy Braddock got up off the canvas to fight one more round all the way to the world championship, he gave down-and-outers everywhere a shot in the arm.

If you are down on the canvas today, it might help you to discover the story behind Jimmy's miracle win. Most folks forget that early on Braddock was a perennial contender. But he always lost to the best boxers. He had a powerful right hand, but his left was weak. Top fighters exploited that weakness to beat him. When he broke his right hand, his career was as good as over. He gamely took on lesser fighters, but he repeatedly broke his right hand because it was his only weapon. Finally, severe arthritis set in to that hand, forcing him to use his left when he went to work as a longshoreman. Day by day, that left hand became increasingly stronger.

Max Baer came into that fight without fear of Braddock's left hand. It turned out to be the cocky champ's fatal mistake on that magical June night in 1935. Sometimes God takes away good things to give us better things. You may be trying to slug it out with your version of a weak left hand. Like Jimmy you've even given up hope that you can ever be a contender again. Don't give up dreams that once gave you hope. Make Jimmy Braddock's credo your own:

*No matter how many times you're knocked down, always get up off the canvas and fight one more round.*

⁂

I have fought the good fight, I have finished
the race, I have kept the faith. Now there is in
store for me the crown of righteousness.

2 TIMOTHY 4:7-8, NIV

# The Man Who Was Bigger Than God

⚜

After his classmates made fun of him, Howie threw away his hearing aids. He lived the rest of his life with an incessant ringing in his ears. It nearly drove him insane. When his prayers for relief went unanswered, he set his credo for life: if you can't depend on God, you have to be your own god.

Fearing the bacteria that bred in the dampness of Houston, his hypochondriac mother sent her son to live in dry Southern California. There, he discovered the two loves of his life: Hollywood and aviation. Lost in the magic of a movie, he forgot the ringing in his ears. Soaring high in an airplane, it stopped altogether.

Then his parents died, making him the world's wealthiest orphan. Howie boasted, "I'm richer than God!" He became the king of Hollywood, producing a string of films. Along the way, he engaged in sexual affairs that led to incurable syphilis. But that didn't stop him from becoming king of the skies or from building history's largest airplane. The world was stunned when he flew to Paris in half the time it took Charles Lindbergh—and then flew around the world in three days. He made a fortune in World War II as the biggest supplier of airplane parts. After he purchased shares in Trans World Airlines, he became the first multibillionaire in history. Howard Hughes now bragged that he was more powerful than God.

Yet his bravado masked his spreading syphilis. His old fear of germs returned with a vengeance. He moved to Las Vegas for the clean air, purchased a hotel and casino, and lived like a hermit in a sanitary bubble on the top floor. His agents bought up the surrounding casinos to extend his safe zone. He spent millions bribing the president to stop nuclear testing in Nevada, lest he be exposed to radiation. He funneled a fortune to the CIA to stop Russia from unleashing biological warfare. Howard Hughes was now the ultimate control freak.

Toward the end, he was downing hundreds of pills every day. He would eat little besides green peas, and he had each one measured so he wouldn't choke to death. He kept a team of doctors on full-time alert, wore surgical gowns, used Kleenex boxes for shoes, and wouldn't allow anything to touch his exposed skin. If a flu or cold epidemic hit the area, a private jet would quickly whisk him away.

In spite of all his precautions, he fell into a coma when he was seventy and died in transit to the hospital on April 5, 1976. He was the richest man in the world, but his six-foot-four-inch frame had been starved down to ninety pounds, his body covered by filth and his arms riddled with holes. X-rays showed broken needles lodged under his skin. The autopsy revealed a brain eaten by syphilis. He was so unrecognizable that the FBI took fingerprints to confirm his identity. The story of a man who thought he was bigger than God screams a warning to all of us who try to control our world. We might relax more if we remember this:

*Worries don't come from thinking about the future but from wanting to control it.*

───── ⣔⣖⣕ ─────

Cast your burden upon the LORD and
He will sustain you; He will never
allow the righteous to be shaken.

PSALM 55:22, NASB

# Strong Heart

~~~

His mother gave him a Latin name that means "strong heart." She knew that her son needed to be strong in a world that was falling apart. Rome was in its death throes, and barbarian Goths were moving south to feed like vultures on its carcass. But Strong Heart grew up to justify the name his mother gave him. As a courageous pastor, this son of wealth brought hope to a terrified Rome. Christians and pagans alike celebrated his outrageous acts of charity. His joy was so contagious that even Rome's rulers turned a blind eye to his preaching.

Then a new emperor rose up to save Rome. Marcus Aurelius Claudius was determined to put an end to the Gothic menace. Every Italian man was conscripted into military service. Single men were forbidden to marry. Married men were prohibited from sleeping with their wives. Claudius wanted every ounce of energy focused on defeating the Goths.

But there were young lovers in Italy. When no one else dared to perform a wedding, lovesick couples found their way to the pastor who was famous for his compassion. Strong Heart defied an emperor and performed hundreds of illegal weddings. Almost all those nuptials ended with new believers' baptisms.

When word of the clandestine ceremonies reached the palace, Strong Heart was dragged before an irate emperor. But his contagious joy softened Claudius's hard heart. Palace observers wrote that the pastor could have walked away a free man had he not pressed Claudius to come to Jesus. Instead, the emperor angrily sentenced him to die.

Death row did nothing to blunt Strong Heart's joy. His jailer was so impressed that he brought his blind daughter to visit the prisoner, hoping that the man's exuberance would pull her out of a lifetime of self-pity. Soon both were laughing, and within days they were in love. On the eve of his execution, the pastor wrote a final love letter to his sweetheart, signing it in a way that is still celebrated today.

At dawn, Strong Heart forgave each of his executioners and implored them to receive Jesus. They repaid his lavish love by beating him so brutally that his great heart exploded. Perhaps that's why a blood-red heart still symbolizes his life.

Scholars long speculated that Strong Heart's story was just another medieval myth. But archaeologists recently uncovered the remains of an ancient church in Rome. Chiseled in its doorway arch are the words of Pope Julius I honoring a man named Strong Heart who died on February 14. You may never have heard of Emperor Claudius, who died of disease around the same time, but today you remember Strong

Heart, whose Latin name was Valentinus, and the way he ended that final letter to his sweetheart: "Your Valentine." Giving your heart away is risky. Too many folks try to protect their heart from hurt. If you are tempted to play it safe with love, remember Saint Valentine's story in light of something Mother Teresa once said:

*If you give until it hurts, there is no more hurt, only love.*

---

A new commandment I give to you, that
you love one another. . . . By this all people
will know that you are my disciples, if
you have love for one another.

JOHN 13:34-35, ESV

# The King of the Mountain

⌒⌒⌒

The descent from the mountaintop can be so painful. Just ask the old boxer. Sportswriter Gary Smith interviewed him on one of the saddest sports specials ever aired. Too many blows to the head in too many fights over too many years had slurred the ex-champ's words. Those closest to him had begged him to get out of the ring, but he refused to stop until his crown was taken from him.

Shuffling and shaking with tremors, the old boxer led the sportswriter to a weathered barn behind his farmhouse. Photos, posters, and portraits showed the ex-champ in his prime, his sculpted arms raised, fists pumping the air, and face glowing with unbridled exuberance. But the pictures were faded and covered with bird droppings. Pigeons now made their home where he had once trained.

Shaking his head in embarrassment, the old champ shuffled slowly to the photos and turned them over one by one. He then limped to the door and stared off into the distance. The silence was eloquently painful in that barn. He turned to Smith and quietly slurred, "I had the world, and it wasn't nothin'. Look now."

Long ago, the champ *did* have the world. Most experts agree that Muhammad Ali was the greatest fighter ever to dance across the ring. He won the world heavyweight championship three times and was the most recognized athlete on the planet. His face appeared on the cover of *Sports Illustrated* more times than any other person. As long as he was floating like a butterfly and stinging like a bee, he commanded the limelight and mesmerized his adoring public with non-stop chatter. An entourage followed in his wake, constantly stroking his king-size ego. Muhammad Ali was "King of the Mountain."

As the interview ended, the champ was clearly worn out. Parkinson's was reducing him to uncontrollable tremors. His daughter said that it was time to take him back to the house. He shuffled out past pictures of "The Thrilla in Manila" and "The Rope-A-Dope in Zaire," now faded and covered with pigeon droppings. It was too painful to watch. Mercifully, the cameras faded to a commercial featuring a new sports superstar plugging a product. But those haunting words still hung in the air: "I had the world, and it wasn't nothin'. Look now."

Most of us know the king of the mountain game. It's as primitive as it is brutal. The object is to get to the top of the pile. So we push, claw, and crawl to stand higher than anyone else. But getting to the top is a dubious victory. Already, those below are trying to topple the king. Be careful when you hang those victory posters. Pigeons are making their nests in the rafters. You can learn a lot from the story of Muhammad Ali. You can learn even more from the king who came down from heaven's mountain as a suffering servant. He became a lamb and ended up the Lion of Judah. The greatest story ever told teaches us this:

*The best way to find yourself is to lose yourself in the service of others.*

༺☙☙༻

The Son of Man came not to be served but to serve others and to give his life as a ransom for many.

MATTHEW 20:28

# Paco's Papa

Ernie felt like God had played a cruel joke on him. Born a free spirit, he was raised in a staid Victorian house on Main Street in a Midwestern town. His mother crammed her religion down his throat, and a perfectionistic father demanded that Ernie excel in everything he did. Ernie felt smothered. He later wrote that he grew up in a town of wide lawns and narrow minds.

His folks wanted him to become a doctor, but he loved to write. After high school he escaped to Kansas City to work for a newspaper. His parents were scandalized, but his editors said that he was a boy genius. His wanderlust led him to join the Red Cross ambulance corps on the Italian front in World War I. It was exhilarating until he was severely wounded. In the hospital he fell in love with a volunteer nurse named Agnes. Ernie returned home to Illinois confident that she would soon join him as his wife.

A few months later, he received a devastating letter. Agnes had fallen in love with someone else. Ernie never got over that rejection. He began to drink heavily. Though a rising star in the literary world, he was gaining a reputation as a barroom brawler. Rage and alcoholism would torment Ernie to the end.

One day Agnes showed up at his father's lake. When he opened the door, she pleaded, "Ernie, please forgive me and take me back!" Without a word, he slammed the door in her face. A few years later, when his father took his own life, Ernie snarled, "Everyone who commits suicide rots in hell." When his mother died, he refused to attend her funeral. Over the years, booze and bitterness dismantled Ernie. He plowed through four marriages. Even though his friends called him Papa, his children lived in fear of his rage. At age sixty-one, he put a shotgun to his head and pulled the trigger.

His family called him Ernie, but the world remembers him as Ernest Hemingway. He wrote novels like *For Whom the Bell Tolls* and *A Farewell to Arms*. He was awarded both the Pulitzer and Nobel Prizes. As a writer, Hemingway was a giant. As a celebrity adventurer, he was bigger than life. But the real Ernie never ceased being the bitter little boy who couldn't do enough to please his parents.

None of Hemingway's stories capture his deep wounds more than the one about Paco. After he wrongs his father, the boy runs away to Madrid. Paco's father follows him to the city. Unable to find Paco, his father takes out a newspaper ad: "Paco, meet me at the Hotel Montana, twelve noon, Tuesday. All is forgiven. Papa." When the father arrives at the hotel, he finds a lobby filled with eight hundred young men, all named Paco.

Ernie captures his and our hearts' longing. Whether we are the Prodigal Son in the far country or the older brother keeping all the rules at home, we want to know that our father loves us unconditionally. What a difference it would have made for Ernest Hemingway—and would make for all of us—to grasp this:

*God loves each of us as if there were only one of us.*

———— ✲ ————

When God our Savior revealed his kindness and love, he saved us, not because of the righteous things we had done, but because of his mercy.

TITUS 3:4-5

# The Hand That Rocks the Cradle

⁓

S ukey was a feminist long before it was fashionable. In an age when girls were raised to please husbands and birth babies, she had bigger dreams. Her doting daddy treated her more like a son than a daughter. While other girls were learning how to cook and sew, he taught her Latin and Greek. When ladies retired to the parlor after dinner, she joined the men in the library.

Because she was allowed to soar intellectually, Sukey set her heart on publishing poetry a century before Jane Austen broke the gender barrier, and she fantasized about being the first woman admitted to Oxford. But her father clipped her wings by forcing her to marry Samuel, a mediocre preacher. She would spend her marriage in rural parishes with country bumpkins.

Their first parish was a dreary village with a mud cottage manse. She gave birth to seven children, only to watch three of them die. A careless midwife maimed the seventh for life. After six difficult pregnancies in eight years, Sukey almost died of exhaustion.

Things looked up when they were called to a richer parish. But Samuel managed money as badly as he preached. When their eighth child was born, he took to the road to earn extra income. He returned home enough times to sire five more children, who all died in infancy. After their manse burned down, Samuel abandoned his family. When he finally returned, Sukey birthed five more babies in rapid succession. He left it to her to educate their passel of kids. Both sons and daughters got as fine an education as the young scholars at Oxford.

When he was sixty-five, Samuel suffered a stroke. Sukey cared for him for seven years while they survived on charity. The feminist who dreamed of publishing poetry spent her life in obscurity. She gave birth to nineteen children, burying eight of them in infancy. Only seven were still alive when she died. You might be tempted to weep for her if you didn't know the rest of her story.

Her daddy nicknamed her Sukey. But history remembers her by her given name, Susanna, the wife of the Reverend Samuel Wesley. One of her sons, John, sparked a great revival in colonial America that birthed the Revolutionary War. Along the way, he founded the Methodist Church. Another son, Charles, penned more than nine thousand poems and hymns. Samuel Jr. became one of England's greatest scholars. Hetty became the poet her mother was never allowed to be. Two other daughters were prominent educators. All of

Sukey's dreams, and so much more, were realized through the children she nurtured and inspired. One might argue that there would be no United States had there been no Susanna Wesley. Certainly, millions owe their spiritual lives to that woman.

Do you see your story in Sukey's disappointments? Have your dreams been dashed or your hopes postponed? Maybe life has deposited you at a wide spot on the road to nowhere. Is it possible that God has placed you here for bigger purposes than you can dare imagine? Take heart from Susanna Wesley's story:

*God's gifts put our best dreams to shame.*

༄༅

"I know the plans I have for you," declares the LORD, "plans to prosper you and not to harm you, plans to give you hope and a future."

JEREMIAH 29:11, NIV

# The Unwanted Boy

ﾟ◦◉◦ﾟ

B enny was born out of wedlock to an immigrant mother who was abandoned by her lover, a country doctor. It wasn't easy being the love child of an unwed mother, especially during the late 1800s in rural Tennessee. Teased unmercifully, he learned to fight back with fists and bulldog tenacity. But his hard-shell exterior masked the shame he felt as the town ragamuffin. Mostly, Benny hated the town gossip about the things his mother did at night to make ends meet.

Sometimes the boy would slip into the church house by himself. His shabby clothes and outcast status caused him to hide in the back pew. Most of the time, he would slip out before the benediction. But that day he waited too long, and the aisle was clogged with people. Benny was unable to avoid the preacher.

He grabbed the boy by the shoulder and said, "You must be the child of . . ." Looking perplexed, he repeated, "You must be the child of . . ." Benny shrank back in embarrassment, figuring that it wouldn't be long before someone chimed in that he was the son of a tramp. But the pastor slapped him on the back and exclaimed, "Now I recognize you. You're a child of God. You go out there and claim your rightful inheritance!"

A few months later, Benny's mother put him in an orphanage, and he was later reunited with his father. With the new opportunities afforded by his doctor daddy and a dogged determination forged in early childhood, Benny did go out and make something of himself. But he would tell everyone that when a Baptist preacher told him to go out and claim his rightful inheritance, it was the turning point in his life.

Years later, Benny was living out his last years in the Tennessee mountains of his childhood. One evening, as he left a restaurant, he passed by a vacationing seminary professor, Dr. Fred Craddock, the professor of preaching at Candler School of Theology in Atlanta. Benny engaged him in some easy mountain banter. When Dr. Craddock told him that he taught young men how to preach, the old man broke into a wide smile. He told the professor about the preacher who inspired him one Sunday morning when he was an unwanted boy. Then he whispered, "You tell your preacher boys that they can change lives by helping folks believe the best things about their future."

As Benny shuffled out of the restaurant, Dr. Craddock asked his waitress, "Do you know who that old man is?" "Everyone knows him," she said. "He's a legend hereabouts. His name is Ben Hooper, the most famous lawyer in this state, and a two-time governor of Tennessee."

You can read Ben Hooper's story in his autobiography, *The Unwanted Boy*. It proves that there is a transforming power in believing the best things. Please don't allow the traumas of childhood, disabilities of adulthood, opinions of others, sins of the past, or your own negative self-talk determine who you are. You are a child of God. Go out and claim your inheritance today! Ben Hooper's triumphant story celebrates this unalterable transforming truth:

*The future you see is most often the future you get.*

⁂

[Jesus said,] "Everything is possible
for one who believes."

MARK 9:23, NIV

# The Godfather and the Priest

❧❧❧

S he was the crown jewel of Europe and the birthplace of the Renaissance. In this magical city, banking families controlled the wealth of the world, Michelangelo created his art, Galileo pondered the movements of the solar system, Dante studied poetry, and Machiavelli tutored princes on how to wield power. Surely, Florence stood at the crossroads of history.

Yet behind the scenes, a puppet master pulled the strings. He was the boss of bosses, the godfather of Florence— Lorenzo the Magnificent, patriarch of the Medici banking cartel and the richest man in Europe. In public, he was a great patron of the arts and church. Because of his largesse, artists like Michelangelo, Botticelli, and Leonardo da Vinci were able to make the world more beautiful. He also bankrolled the soaring cathedrals that made Florence the envy of Christendom.

But anyone who scratched beneath the thin veneer of Renaissance beauty would find Lorenzo's Florence to be a Hollywood spectacular of decadence and drag, prostitutes and political graft, where nothing and nobody could be trusted. Lorenzo supported an unspeakably corrupt pope in order to elevate his own nephew, Giulio, to the papacy. At Lorenzo's insistence, the pope made fourteen-year-old Giulio a cardinal. When Giulio later became pope, he would fill offices of the church with hoodlums from the Medici family and would make the Vatican treasury his personal piggy bank.

Yet during Lorenzo's age of gilded decadence, a reformer rose in Florence—the Dominican friar Girolamo Savonarola. This firebrand thundered against the worldliness of Florentine Christians and exposed church corruption. Some fifteen thousand people regularly packed the great cathedral in Florence to hear him preach. Repentant people brought their opulence to the city square to be burned in what Savonarola called "the bonfires of the vanities." This Renaissance "John the Baptist" called for Lorenzo to repent and the Borgia pope, Alexander, to step down.

The Borgias reacted with fury. Pope Alexander excommunicated Savonarola. His son, Cesare, rushed to Florence to orchestrate the friar's burning at the stake. Shortly before his martyrdom, Savonarola gave an amazing prophecy: "It matters little what you do to me today. Within forty years a man will rise up in the north to bring a reformation that can't be stopped." Some twenty years later, during the papacy of Lorenzo's son, Martin Luther rose in the north country of Germany to spark a reformation that couldn't be stopped. Today Lorenzo the Magnificent lies forgotten in an ornate tomb while simple friars and monks like Savonarola and Luther are celebrated. Not far from Lorenzo's mausoleum, a vendor sells a T-shirt that the godfather of Florence, the Borgia gang, and the corrupt popes would despise. But Savonarola and Luther would probably buy and wear the shirt with this slogan:

*Your ego is not your amigo.*

---

When they saw the courage of Peter and
John and realized that they were unschooled,
ordinary men, they were astonished and they
took note that these men had been with Jesus.

ACTS 4:13, NIV

# The Leper Who Became a Saint

⟨◦◦⟩

W who could have imagined that Jozef would one day be canonized as a saint? As the seventh child of a poor coin collector, he got the family leftovers. He didn't have access to much education, and he did poorly in school. But he had a heart for the underdog. No one was surprised when Jozef applied to be a priest. Nor were they shocked that he was initially rejected as uneducated and unintelligent. When he applied to be a missionary, he was turned down as unsuitable. Only after they couldn't find anyone else to go did they finally send him.

Jozef arrived in Hawaii in 1864, during a year of great panic. Leprosy had found its way to paradise, and it was spreading like wildfire among native Polynesians. Protestant missionaries said that this was God's judgment on the licentious lifestyle of the islanders. American planters threatened to seize the islands by armed force if something wasn't done.

Lepers were rounded up and shipped to a deserted peninsula on Molokai Island. It was isolated and windswept, accessible only by a mule trail over steep mountains. The lepers might as well have been dumped on the moon. In this place of sorrow, they waited to die in ramshackle huts amidst filthy squalor. A few Protestant missionaries and Catholic priests visited, but most quickly left.

About that time, Jozef remembered his ordination as a priest. His superiors had covered him with a funeral pall to symbolize his death to the world. When he begged his bishop to go to the leper colony as its resident priest, he was signing his death warrant. When he left for Molokai, he knew he was never coming back. Outside of Jesus, no one ever loved lepers more than Jozef. He built a church with his own hands, dug a reservoir, founded a school, and brought stability. He made coffins and dug the graves for six hundred lepers. Maybe he loved them too much when he kissed them on their lips, shared his tobacco pipe with them, and dipped his fingers in their poi—a traditional dish made of mashed taro root. But he cared more about the outcasts than he did about hygiene. It wasn't long before he turned a place of sorrow into a sanctuary of hope.

A decade after he arrived, he accidently put his foot in scalding water. When he saw the blisters but felt no pain, he immediately sent word to his superiors, "I have leprosy. Please send a confessor." He ministered four more years while his body was eaten away. In his last weeks he wrote a letter to his brother: "I thank God very much for letting me die of the same disease and in the same way as my lepers." The world remembers Jozef by the name he took when he became a priest, Father Damien. When he died, church bells rang in mourning across the islands. Every year, Hawaiians celebrate the memory of this Belgian priest. In 2009, he was canonized as Saint Damien. He is called the patron saint of those with leprosy, HIV, and AIDS. His service to the sick and outcast continues to be a source of inspiration to people worldwide. When we are reluctant to identify with those Jesus called "the least of these," we might want to remember this:

*Each sick and outcast person is really Jesus in disguise.*

⁓

The King will say, "I tell you the truth, when
you did it to one of the least of these my brothers
and sisters, you were doing it to me!"

MATTHEW 25:40

# A Victory in Defeat

❧❧❧

The east was on a collision course with the west in 480 BC. The world watched in awe as the largest army in history poured into Europe. Heading this colossal war machine was Xerxes, the king of Persia. His army numbered almost two million foot soldiers, eighty thousand horsemen, twenty thousand chariots, camel-riding Arabs, and war elephants from India. Xerxes had crafted the most lethal weapon of mass destruction that humankind had ever seen. The Greek historian Herodotus wrote that when this beast from the east marched, the ground shook. When it stopped to drink, pools were dried up and rivers reduced to a trickle.

You may remember Xerxes as the husband of the biblical heroine Esther. This self-proclaimed "king of kings" spent four years amassing his titanic force to crush tiny Greece. It was the mismatch of the ages. Greece was a collection of city-states warring against each other. Athens was mired in social stagnation, and Sparta was in economic shambles. Never was a nation so vulnerable. Yet five Greek cities managed to scrape together about five thousand soldiers. They were outnumbered 430 to 1. But at their core were three hundred

Spartans. These three hundred had been trained since childhood to stand or die in battle. Every Spartan mother sent her sons off to war with this warning: "Come home with your shield, or on it."

The Greeks took their stand in a narrow pass, fifty feet wide, with the sea on one side and towering cliffs on the other, at a place called Thermopylae. This battleground has become hallowed in military history. It is to the Greeks what the Alamo is to Texans. In that narrow pass a heroic handful held back the Persian hordes for two days. When Xerxes finally unleashed his crack stormtroopers, the Greeks annihilated them. But on the third night, a traitor showed the Persians a secret trail through the cliffs into Thermopylae. Sure death was coming with the breaking dawn. Dismissing the rest of the Greeks, General Leonidas led his three hundred Spartans, along with some loyal Thespians, to a mound where they made their final stand. When their weapons were gone, they fought with hands and teeth until the last man died. As the end neared, a runner was sent home with the message that still echoes down the corridors of time: "Stranger, tell the Spartans that we behaved as they would wish us to, and are buried here."

This small band of Spartans died without knowing they were changing history. They bought enough time for the Greek cities to raise a great army. Their heroism triggered a surge of national pride that led to decisive victories at Salamis and Plataea. The power of Persia was broken. The future of civilization shifted from Asia to Europe. Athens became the world's most influential city. Greek culture and democracy would give birth to the modern world. Maybe you are facing overwhelming odds. Perhaps you have suffered a crushing defeat. Take heart from the story of three hundred Spartans. Surely it teaches us a valuable lesson:

*There are some defeats whose triumphs rival victories.*

⎯⎯⎯ ⎆⊙⊙⊙ ⎯⎯⎯

Some nations boast of their chariots and horses, but we boast in the name of the LORD our God. Those nations will fall down and collapse, but we will rise up and stand firm.

PSALM 20:7-8, NIV

# One Last Song in a Tattered Coat

❧

There was a time that he had written songs that made the whole world sing. Now he was just another drunken bum in the Bowery, ravaged with fever and starving to death. On a cold winter's morning, this shell of a man staggered out of his bed and stumbled to the public washbasin in a cheap flophouse. He fell and shattered the sink. They found him naked and incoherent, bleeding from a deep gash in his throat. A quack doctor was called to the scene. He used a string of black sewing thread to suture the wound. All the time the bum begged for a drink. A buddy shared the bottom of a bottle of cheap rum to dull his pain.

The bum was dumped into a police paddy wagon and dropped off at Bellevue Hospital, where he was left on a dirty gurney in the charity ward. He languished for three days without food or attention before he finally gasped his last breath. No one cared that a homeless drunk from the Bowery had died.

A friend came looking for him in the morgue. He found the body among rows of other nameless corpses with "John

Doe" tags on their toes. When the friend gathered the man's meager belongings, he found a tattered coat with a few cents in one pocket and a scrap of paper in the other. Five words were scribbled on it: "Dear friends and gentle hearts." As the friend looked at these words, he wondered if they were the beginnings of a song.

Why would a Bowery bum carry around a line of lyrics? Could it be that he still believed he had the old magic? Was it possible that the heart of a genius still beat faintly in the emaciated body of a derelict? After all, there was a time long ago when he had written more than two hundred songs that are indelibly etched in our American heritage. Every schoolchild has sung his most famous songs: "Camptown Races," "Oh! Susanna," "My Old Kentucky Home," "Beautiful Dreamer," and "Jeanie with the Light Brown Hair." Who would have guessed that the Bowery bum was Stephen F. Foster, the most prolific songwriter in American history?

Is there anyone who is beyond redemption? At the dead end of his life, the father of American music still carried a scrap of hope in his tattered coat pocket. Every life, no matter how battered, still carries a scrap of hope and a melody waiting to be reborn. Some are in hospitals, others in nursing homes, and still others in prisons. Others are unwanted children in their mothers' wombs, but they still have a song to sing. Still others are people who slip into church each Sunday, but they are too discouraged to sing a song. Have the songs in your soul been silenced by the adversities of life? Don't lose heart. You still have songs locked in your soul, waiting to be written. Remember Stephen Foster's story in the light of this line from the blind hymn writer Fanny Crosby:

*Chords that were broken will vibrate once more.*

&#8766;

Let the ruins of Jerusalem break into joyful song, for the LORD has comforted his people. He has redeemed Jerusalem.

ISAIAH 52:9

# From Africa with Love

୧ଶ୬୬

There was once an African queen who heard about a powerful king in faraway Asia. She was told so many tall tales about this king that she found it impossible to restrain her curiosity. So she left her Ethiopian palace and embarked on a long journey. When she arrived in the fabled Asian kingdom, the queen came face-to-face with the world's richest man.

His lifestyle still boggles our imagination three thousand years later. He sat on a throne of pure ivory overlaid with gold. The plates and goblets at his lavish banquets were made of pure gold. Every morning he dressed in snow-white robes to ride out in a chariot made of the finest cedar, inlaid with gold and ivory, carpeted in tapestries woven with gold thread, and pulled by the finest horses on earth. A bodyguard of sixty warriors accompanied him: the tallest and handsomest men in his kingdom, arrayed in Tyrian purple, each with long black hair sprinkled daily with fresh gold dust.

His vast estates included parks, zoos, temples, libraries, universities, and lavish resorts. A thousand delights awaited him in his palace of pleasures: the world's most beautiful women, orchestras, choirs, singers, dancers, magicians, and circus acts to rival the Cirque du Soleil.

This hedonist was also the greatest thinker in antiquity. His court was filled with the brightest of scholars who traveled across the globe to learn from his renowned wisdom. He wrote four books that are among the towering classics in history, and he composed wise sayings that are still repeated today, as well as three thousand poems and more than one thousand songs. As a military strategist, he had no peer. His unparalleled skills at diplomacy achieved peace in the Middle East.

After spending months with the Asian king, the African queen gushed, "All that I heard is not even half of what I have seen." You remember this Ethiopian queen by her kingdom's ancient name, Sheba. The Asian king was Solomon. The Ethiopian left with memories to last several lifetimes. Some believe she also carried Solomon's baby in her womb, which would mean all of her descendants, including the last emperor of Ethiopia, Haile Selassie, carried Solomon's DNA. The Queen of Sheba also brought Judaism to Ethiopia. A thousand years later, an official of the Ethiopian royal court traveled to Jerusalem to worship at the Temple. On the way home, a church deacon told him about Jesus and baptized him. The court official brought Christianity back to Africa, making the Ethiopian Orthodox Church the oldest continuing Christian body in the world—all this because a curious African queen decided to visit an Asian king!

The king wrote a biblical love story called the Song of Solomon. Many scholars believe that he was writing about his love affair with the African queen. But it is also an allegorical story of God's love for his people. Having read the story of an African queen and her Israelite lover, you might want to read the Song of Solomon to see how passionately the king of heaven loves you. Those who have already embraced this king will agree with this:

*What you have heard about Jesus is not half of what there is to see.*

⟡

I didn't believe what was said until I arrived here and saw it with my own eyes. In fact, I had not heard the half of it!

1 KINGS 10:7

# The Folly of Unnecessary Battles

c⊙⊙⊙

The largest battle ever fought on American soil began with a search for shoes. Before the butchery ended, it had exacted fifty-one thousand casualties. It was the worst slaughter in our history.

Historians now agree that the battle should not have been fought. If only the commanding general of the Army of Northern Virginia had read *The Art of War* by Sun Tzu, a single principle espoused by that Chinese warlord might have stopped him dead in his tracks: "There are roads which must not be followed, armies which must not be attacked."

But General Robert E. Lee had set out on a desperate gamble to turn the tide of a war that was going from bad to worse. If the Confederacy could win a major victory, England and France might be willing to throw their much-needed support behind the Southern cause.

Lee's troops broke out of the Shenandoah Valley and marched north toward Philadelphia. But an army marches on shoes, and many of General Lee's ragged Confederates were marching barefoot. In late June, scouts reported that there was a supply of boots at Gettysburg. Lee moved quickly toward the Pennsylvania town. But Gettysburg stood at a junction of ten roads. It's not surprising that Lee's army ran smack-dab into General George Meade's Army of the Potomac.

As the sun dawned on July 3, 1863, Lee held all the cards. He had caught Meade's Union army out of position. His army could either take the open road to an undefended Philadelphia or move south unchallenged to attack Washington, DC. Either way, he could strike a blow that would change the tide of war.

Yet Robert E. Lee inexplicably attacked Meade's army at Gettysburg, even though the Union forces were larger and better armed, and controlled the high ground. At first, Lee's old magic worked. Then his cavalry under Jeb Stuart went on a wild-goose chase. When he lost Stuart, General Lee lost his eyes. Unable to follow Meade's troop movements, he was outmaneuvered.

His generals begged him to retreat, but pride got the best of Lee. He ordered fifteen thousand men to march across a mile of open field against Federals dug in on Cemetery Ridge. Leading the Southern charge was General Pickett's infantry. Two-thirds of Pickett's men were mowed down in a senseless slaughter. Among them were three generals, eight of ten officers above the rank of captain, and three thousand soldiers. The rebels suffered six thousand casualties in a single hour. Pickett later complained, "That old man killed my boys." The shattered Army of Northern Virginia retreated in disgrace, and the sun began to set on the Confederate cause.

Sun Tzu was right: there are some armies that should never be fought. Wasted battles dissipate our strength on lesser things. Robert E. Lee's folly at Gettysburg reminds us to think well before we waste precious resources on labors and battles that give little in return. Maybe our story will turn out better if we remember something Coach John Wooden once said:

***Don't mistake activity with achievement.***

———— ✿ ————

Always give yourselves fully to the work
of the Lord, because you know that your
labor in the Lord is not in vain.

1 CORINTHIANS 15:58, NIV

# The Dangling Telephone

౿౭౹ఎల

They found her cold body tangled in sheets. A telephone receiver dangled from a cord by the bed. Detectives concluded that she had tried to make one last call. Folks in her hometown always said that the Mortenson girl would end up dead before her time.

Actually, she really wasn't the Mortenson girl. No one knew the identity of her real daddy. She was only six when her mother, Gladys, was carted off to the insane asylum, leaving her to be shuffled through too many foster homes, where she was abused and mistreated. In one of these homes, a renter molested her and then purred, "Here, honey, take this nickel and don't tell anyone what I did to you." She later complained, "I found out early on that I was only worth five cents." Even after she grew up to be a Hollywood goddess, she saw herself as little more than a sex object.

She often said, "I want to be loved for myself." Yet Norma Jeane Mortenson constantly reinvented herself. As a child she adopted her mother's maiden name and became Norma Jean Baker. When she married at age sixteen, she was Norma Jean Dougherty. Later she wed a baseball legend and turned into Norma Jean DiMaggio. During her short marriage to a renowned playwright she was Norma Jean Miller. But it was as a twenty-year-old model that a Hollywood publicist gave Norma Jean her most famous name, Marilyn Monroe.

Though she parlayed her sexy blonde persona into mega-stardom, she always felt used and dirty, like a molested little girl. Maybe that's why she plowed through three failed marriages and unhappy romances with the most powerful men in the world. She lamented, "I'm just a small-town girl in a big world trying to find someone to love." Toward the end of her short life, she observed, "A wise girl kisses but doesn't love, listens but doesn't believe, and leaves before she is left."

At age thirty-six, her life was out of control. In desperation, she called an actor friend. After listening to her talk incessantly about how unloved she felt, he impatiently hung up. Popping lethal barbiturates, she frantically tried to call someone who would listen. The next morning, the phone was found dangling by her deathbed.

The editor of *Vogue*, Clare Boothe Luce, later wrote a poignant piece on Norma Jean's death. She asked, "What really killed this love goddess who never found love?" Ms. Luce believed the answer was in that dangling phone. "Marilyn Monroe died because she never got through to someone who would love her."

In his haunting tribute to Norma Jean, "Candle in the Wind," Elton John sang, "Loneliness was tough, the toughest role you ever played." It's the hardest role that any of us ever play. Clare Boothe Luce concluded, "Millions of people are trying to get through to someone who will love them." There is someone who loved us enough to step out of heaven and die on a cross to open the lines of communication. This ought to give you the confidence to pick up the receiver.

*He's been there all the time, waiting patiently on the line.*

⁂

Call to me and I will answer you, and will tell you great and hidden things that you have not known.

JEREMIAH 33:3, ESV

# Christianity in Shoe Leather

࿇

Not much ever happened in little Northfield, Massachusetts. Who would have guessed that one of its ragged orphans would change the world? Lyman was only four when his daddy worked himself into an early grave. By the time he was seventeen, he could barely read or write. With two dollars in his pocket, he headed for Boston to work in his uncle's boot shop.

His pious uncle asked him to promise to go to church on Sundays. But the unschooled teen struggled with the big words in the sermons. He invariably fell asleep. Fortunately, a Sunday school teacher took an interest in the slow learner and led him to Jesus. When church elders heard the news, they shook their heads and declared that Lyman would be of little use to God's Kingdom.

Soon afterward, he moved to Chicago to sell shoes. What he lacked in book learning and social graces he made up for in dogged determination, becoming the Windy City's best shoe salesman. He also joined a church where he irritated everyone with his unpolished zeal. His butchered grammar and fractured theology became wildly unpopular. Finally, a delegation of elders advised the shoe salesman, "Leave praying and speaking to those who can do it better."

So Lyman went to the slums of Chicago to set up a Sunday school. People joked that he was too ignorant to teach even unschooled street kids. Yet by sheer tenacity, he dragged thousands of ragged children to his Sunday school. His venture was so successful that it attracted a lawyer from nearby Springfield. Abraham Lincoln often spoke about the Sunday when he watched "legions of ragamuffin kids study the Bible."

Then the shoe salesman started his own church. Mostly, he attracted unschooled hicks. When his church was destroyed in the Great Fire of 1871, he teamed up with a gospel singer and became a traveling evangelist. His poor preaching made him the nation's laughingstock. He spoke so fast that folks couldn't follow. A reporter held a stopwatch and counted his words. Lyman topped out at 230 words a minute. He also topped the scales at four hundred pounds of weight!

But this obese shoe salesman was determined to get the gospel out by any means. Who would have figured that he would personally lead more than a million people to Christ? Or that he would earn the title Prince of Evangelists? No one expected someone with his lackluster background to establish the largest Bible college in America, one of the world's biggest publishing houses, and a string of schools that sent five thousand missionaries overseas during his lifetime, making America the largest missionary-sending nation in history!

The world remembers him by his full name, Dwight Lyman Moody. There's not a Christian in the world that hasn't been affected by that shoe salesman. D. L. Moody proves that none of us are so devoid of talent that we can't do so much more, if only we would take up the challenge that spurred him to greatness:

*The world has yet to see what God can do with a person fully consecrated to him.*

---

[Jesus said,] "Very truly I tell you, whoever believes
in me will do the works I have been doing, and
they will do even greater things than these."

JOHN 14:12, NIV

# Be Careful Little Eyes
# What You See

⚜

L ittle Theodore never felt like he belonged. It would be years before he figured out why. By then his rage was off the charts.

His teen mother named him Theodore Robert Cowell, giving him her maiden name. She took her baby to Philadelphia to live with his grandparents. Ashamed of being an unwed mother, she told her son that she was his sister. He would be an adult before he discovered that his "big sister" was really his mother, and that his grandparents weren't Mom and Dad. He never forgave that deception.

When he was four, his mom took him from the only home he had ever known and moved across the country. Theodore never recovered from the trauma of that move or the fact that his mother was incapable of showing affection. To make matters worse, she married an abusive alcoholic. The boy withdrew into a shell of bitter loneliness. Though he grew up to be quite handsome, Theodore had few friends or dates. He could never shake his paranoid fear of intimacy.

At age twelve, he found some porn magazines in a garbage

dump. Through soft porn he tried to connect with women without risking intimacy. But the flesh is never satisfied. So Theodore graduated to the hard stuff. He tried to break his addiction by incessantly repeating a mantra he learned in Sunday school: "Be careful little eyes what you see." But he couldn't overcome the weaknesses of his flesh.

After the only girl he ever loved broke up with him, Theodore snapped. Somewhere outside Seattle, he killed his first victim. Before he was finished, he became the most prolific murderer in US history. Some experts say that he may have tortured and murdered as many as one hundred women in a cross-country killing spree. On the night before he was strapped into the electric chair at the Florida State Prison, Theodore "Ted" Bundy confessed to Dr. James Dobson,

> There was an unfulfilled longing in my heart. I thought that pornography could fill the emptiness. My mind was always focused on the wrong things. They became the doorways that allowed sinister spirits to come inside me. Violence became part of my fantasies. I drank lots of alcohol to reduce my religious inhibitions. When I committed my first murder it seemed like I was possessed by something awful and alien.

Ted Bundy spent the last night of his life praying with a minister. He wept over the horror and pain he had inflicted on his victims. In the early morning hours, Theodore finally smiled and said, "My eyes will soon see something beautiful for the first time." What will you look at today? Herman Melville wrote, "Eyes are windows to the soul." If you recall Ted's story, you might take this truth seriously:

*Eyes are glass doors through which the visible world enters to take control of the invisible soul.*

⚬⚬⚬

Your eye is like a lamp that provides light for your body. When your eye is healthy, your whole body is filled with light. But when your eye is unhealthy, your whole body is filled with darkness.

MATTHEW 6:22-23

# A Tale of Two Families

୧୭୭୭

This amazing story of two families spans several generations. Both trace their lineage back to two men who
lived in colonial America. One called himself Jukes. But his
name isn't so important. He was constantly coming up with
a new alias to stay a step ahead of the law. Jukes was, according to his neighbors, "a shiftless, lazy no-account." The little
that he managed to scrape together was mostly gained by his
marginal skills as a petty thief. But Mr. Jukes was never clever
enough to outwit the local sheriff. He was constantly in and
out of jail. His wife was a woman of low morals who spent
too much time in a drunken stupor.

At the turn of the twentieth century, a series of sociolo-
gists managed to uncover twelve hundred descendants in the
Jukes family tree. Some three hundred were professional beg-
gars. More than a hundred were convicted criminals. Sixty
were thieves and pickpockets. At least four hundred of them
were drunkards or drug addicts. Another seven were convicted murderers, although several more were suspects. More
than fifty of them spent time in mental institutions. Of the
twelve hundred descendants discovered by the educators,

only twenty ever learned a trade. Half who did learned their trade in prison. Less than two hundred of Jukes's descendants finished high school, and none attended college. The Jukeses' family record was one of pauperism and prison, imbecility and insanity, prostitution and panhandling, drunkenness and drug abuse.

One sociologist also studied the family tree of a colonial contemporary of Jukes. He was a preacher, as were his father and grandfather. Scholars say that he was the greatest theologian and philosopher ever produced by America. His dynamic preaching sparked a great spiritual awakening that birthed the American Revolution. Maybe you remember this third president of Princeton, the Reverend Jonathan Edwards, and his famous sermon "Sinners in the Hands of an Angry God." But you may not have ever shaken his family tree to see what fell out.

A total of four hundred descendants have been traced to Jonathan Edwards and his wife, Sarah. Among them was a US vice president, three US senators, three governors, three mayors, thirteen college and university presidents, and thirty judges. Around sixty-five of Edwards's progeny were college professors. Another hundred were ministers, missionaries, or seminary professors. Eighty were public office holders. In his family tree were one hundred lawyers and sixty medical doctors. Several descendants had written books, published newspapers, or been editors of journals. Until the beginning of the twentieth century, every major industry in America had as its founder or promoter an offspring of Jonathan and Sarah Edwards.

Most families are mixed bags of success and failures. Few are as dismal as Jukes's descendants, or as stellar as Edwards's progeny. But the contrast cannot be missed, nor the lesson dismissed. Parents have a profound impact on their world for generations to come. Nothing is more important than the responsibilities and possibilities of parenthood. The story of two families shouts a message:

*Your children will become who you are, so be who you want them to be.*

⎯⎯⎯ ༄ ⎯⎯⎯

Direct your children onto the right path, and
when they are older, they will not leave it.

PROVERBS 22:6

# Feathers in the Wind

&#8450;&#8476;&#8450;

H e was on a business trip when his heart was broken. As he looked across the dining room, he saw his pastor. Why was the good reverend in this restaurant so far from home? As he hurried across the room to greet the pastor, he froze in his tracks. His pastor was with a woman who wasn't his wife, and they were holding hands by candlelight.

The businessman felt like a bomb had gone off in his face. Then he remembered that he was an elder with an obligation to protect the flock from a wolf in sheep's clothing. His first reaction was to confront his philandering pastor. But he didn't want to create a scene. So he fled to his hotel room and called his wife. She was quick with advice. He needed to call an emergency meeting of the elders. He hung up his phone and began to pack. She picked up hers and began to call her friends. The news spread like wildfire. By the next day, the two-timing pastor was the talk of the town. By evening, clergy several states away had heard about the affair. A "concerned" friend informed the pastor's wife. Her husband returned home to a full-blown scandal. He protested his innocence, but the genie was out of the bottle.

By week's end the church auditorium was packed for a congregational meeting that was more like a public hanging. Hardly anyone noticed the pretty blonde. They were more captivated by the reverend and his tight-lipped family as they walked down the aisle. A hush fell over the crowd as he stepped into his pulpit. The assembled vultures expected a public confession. Instead, he said, "I have come to tender my resignation. My family is deeply wounded, and my reputation soiled. In choosing to believe the worst, you have done things that cannot be undone." He then stepped down to the front row and took the hand of the pretty blonde. "I'd like to introduce you to my baby sister. She is the woman who was in the restaurant with me. Her husband had just left her, and I drove three hundred miles to bring comfort." With that, he and his family walked out past a stunned congregation.

In the days that followed, frantic knocking on his front door went unanswered. Phone calls were not returned. As the movers went about their work, parishioners stood in the driveway and pled with the pastor to stay. He finally picked up a pillow, tore it open, and shook the feathers into the wind. "If you can find and return all these feathers, and if every word of gossip can be returned to your mouths unsaid, then things can be made right again."

This true account is told with the names of pastor and church kept secret to protect hearts still fragile and broken years later. This story of a rush to judgment should remind all of us to be careful about what we assume to be true. We will be even more careful not to spread gossip or slander if we remember this:

*We reveal the most about ourselves when we speak about others.*

⁂

Do not judge others, and you will not be judged. For you will be treated as you treat others. The standard you use in judging is the standard by which you will be judged.

MATTHEW 7:1-2

# The Unlikely Leader

e☙❦❧ఎ

If Jimmy could make it, anyone could. Rejected by his parents and shunned by his schoolmates, he retreated into a lonely world of self-loathing. His only comfort was stuffing himself with food until he became grotesquely obese. His flabby white face was covered with pimples and scarred with acne. He reeked of body odor and stuttered whenever he opened his mouth.

One day everything changed for this social outcast. As he walked down a London side street, he looked into a doorway and saw a ragtag collection of fellow losers seated on folding chairs. A sign told him that this was the meeting hall of the Communist Party. A well-dressed man greeted him warmly with this line: "No matter who you are, we can turn you into a leader of men."

Jimmy took the seat closest to the door. The speaker was Douglas Hyde, the editor of the Communist newspaper the *Daily Worker*. Hyde concluded his mesmerizing speech with a bold claim: "I don't care who you are, if you give yourself to the Communist Party, we will turn you into a leader." A tiny seed of hope was planted in Jimmy's heart. He waddled to the podium and stuttered, "C-c-c-comrade, I w-w-w-want you to t-t-turn me into a l-l-leader of m-m-men."

Hyde later wrote in his book, *Dedication and Leadership*, that he groaned within. He had never seen sorrier human material. But he had made a promise. So he gulped and welcomed Jimmy into the brotherhood. The new convert was sent out to the mean streets of London to hand out the *Daily Worker*. He was ridiculed, spit upon, and assaulted. When he returned with his soul battered and bruised, he whimpered, "I c-c-can't d-d-do it!" But his comrades wouldn't let him give up. Slowly but inexorably, Jimmy was transformed from a loser into a leader. The despairing stutterer became a dynamic speaker. The former recluse became the greatest union organizer the Communist Party of Great Britain had ever seen. Years later, his death was front-page news. Factories shut down as thousands attended his funeral.

There is a postscript to Jimmy's story. It has to do with Douglas Hyde, the man who first gave him hope. Hyde left the Communist Party and embraced Christianity. He believed that Christ offered more hope than did Lenin. But when Hyde wrote *Dedication and Leadership* in 1956, disillusionment with the church was setting in—in particular, the Pope's harsh treatment of those on the political left. Hyde said that although Communists believe humans are soulless products of evolution, they often have more faith in their message to transform people than do most Christians. By the time he died in 1966, he had moved away from organized religion. On his deathbed he declared himself to be an "agnostic Christian."

How tragic! Douglas Hyde looked at the church of Jesus rather than the Jesus of the church. Jesus took twelve losers who were misfits like Jimmy Reid and transformed them to change the world. He still does that two thousand years later. If we remember this truth, we will never lose heart in what he can do for us and others:

*God formed us. Sin deformed us. Jesus will transform us.*

---

Anyone who belongs to Christ has become a new person. The old life is gone; a new life has begun!

2 CORINTHIANS 5:17

# A Frog Who Married a Queen

ᴄ◎◉◎ᴅ

It wasn't easy finding Larry. The reporter had to comb through county records and then drive down a dusty road through rusty gates to a ramshackle house. Who would have figured that Larry would fall so far so fast?

Some twenty years earlier, he had been the toast of Hollywood celebrities at Michael Jackson's Neverland Ranch. He might have been a blue-collar builder whose total assets amounted to a few tools and a pickup truck, but on that magical day he was ruggedly handsome—Joe Six-Pack in a J. C. Penney suit, living a fairy tale; the frog who marries a silver-screen queen.

There would be no fairy-tale ending for Larry. Twenty years later he was bloated, bleary eyed, and out of money. Alcohol had reduced him to a shadow of the man who once traveled the world in private jets and on luxury yachts with Hollywood royalty. His memory was fading and his words were slurred.

He showed off a few trinkets from his marriage to the Hollywood queen. He was especially proud of the wedding photo. She looked stunning in her $25,000 dress, and he was handsome in his off-the-rack suit. He looked like the cat that swallowed the canary. In reality, he was the canary who was about to be eaten by the cat and spat out five years later.

This was not a marriage made in heaven. The carpenter totaled his truck while driving drunk. A judge committed him to the Betty Ford Clinic. There he met the movie queen who was there to get clean. After a quick romance, the two got hitched. This was his third marriage and her eighth. She often boasted, "I've only slept with men I'm married to." But she quickly tired of each husband. She once said, "The excitement is in the getting, not the keeping."

The Neverland Ranch marriage was the first time that Elizabeth Taylor married a frog like Larry Fortensky. She said to her wedding guests, "I've finally found a man who can keep me happy." Larry grinned like a Cheshire cat, kidding himself that he could accomplish what a hotel mogul, movie stars, and a US senator had failed to do. It wouldn't be long before she would give him the boot too.

When the reporter finished the interview, Larry sat hunched over in a daze. Maybe he was lost in a dream of what could have been. Or he was thinking about his only daughter who hadn't spoken to him for years because of a fight over money from his divorce settlement. Or perhaps he was looking at his reflection in the mirror behind that wedding photo, seeing how much he had deteriorated since that day at the Neverland Ranch. As the reporter got up to leave, Larry whispered, "Divorce makes you a lot less than you used to be." Divorce seldom makes anyone bigger. If you are ready to bail out of a tough marriage, you might want to remember Larry's story. It screams a warning to couples everywhere:

*Divorce is like an amputation. You may survive, but there's less of you.*

꩜

[Jesus] said, "'This explains why a man leaves his father and mother and is joined to his wife, and the two are united into one.' Since they are no longer two but one, let no one split apart what God has joined together."

MATTHEW 19:5-6

# Sermons from the Crypt

❧

His German name was Karl der Grosse. At age twenty-nine, he was crowned the ruler of a tiny kingdom in what is now modern-day France. Few people at his coronation thought that King Karl would one day reshape the map of Europe.

At the time of Karl's ascension in 771, Europe was a collection of petty fiefdoms, plagued by superstition and ignorance, poverty and pestilence. In the south, Islamic armies had conquered Spain. Vikings were raiding from the north. Ruthless hordes were riding in on the winds of the east.

In this apocalyptic age, Karl rose up to rescue Christendom. Standing six foot four inches tall in a day when the average European stood five foot three, this giant of a man declared war on all those who opposed Christendom. By sheer brutality, he dragged Europe out of the Dark Ages. Over the next forty-two years he fought fifty-three wars. When he defeated an army or captured a city, he insisted that everyone convert to Christianity. Those who refused were slaughtered. After one battle 4,500 Saxons were beheaded when they refused baptism. Their wives and children were driven into a river and drowned. After that, no one dared to oppose Karl's evangelism by intimidation.

By the cross and sword, he carved out an empire that went from the Atlantic to Russia, earning the nickname the Scourge of Christ. Then he spent his final years building monasteries and universities, trying to atone for his reign of terror. He died as one of the most powerful men in the world, outliving four wives and leaving behind five mistresses, eighteen children, and a united Europe.

Two centuries later, workmen accidentally broke into Karl's burial crypt under the cathedral in Aachen, Germany. As they peered into the musty darkness, they saw a two-hundred-year-old skeleton encased in cobwebs and tied with rotting ropes to a throne. Bones were covered with the tatters of what was once a rich robe, now eaten away by time. A crown was perched sideways on a grinning skull.

As the workers inched closer to the macabre remains of the man who once ruled Europe, they saw a table holding a large Bible. The right index finger of the skeleton was resting on a verse in the open book. The workmen called for a priest. Holding a candle close to the Bible, he read the Latin verse of Jesus' words: "What do you benefit if you gain the whole world but lose your own soul?" (Mark 8:36).

Historians recall that on Christmas Day in the year 800, a grateful Pope Leo III gave Karl der Grosse a new name: Carolus Magnus or Charles the Great. History remembers him by a single name, Charlemagne. Each of us has been shaped by the way he transformed history. Yet as he coughed out his last words from a blood-drenched silk pillow, he ordered his body to be buried in a way that would give a message: both the great and small will appear equally naked before God to give an account for their lives down here. We might all want to remember the last sermon preached by an emperor's skeletal remains:

*The only judgment that ultimately matters is the Final Judgment.*

---

He is coming to judge the earth. He will judge the world with justice and the nations with fairness.

PSALM 98:9

# The Magnificent Fraud

∼⊙⊙∼

After an epic battle, Shah Jahan was the undisputed master of a vast subcontinent. Yet it was a hollow victory. His wife had just died in childbirth. For nineteen years the princess of Persia had been his soul mate. Their love was the stuff of storybook legend. In an age when Asian kings kept their wives in harems, she was his chief adviser. She even rode by his side into battle.

His grief was monumental. Those who heard his anguished howling were sure that he had gone mad. When he emerged from his chambers, his courtiers and servants gasped in horror. In only eight days his black hair had turned white. He demanded that his subjects join him in mourning. Those caught smiling in public were executed. The shah's sorrow reduced his vast kingdom to a place of utter desolation.

Then he turned his grief into a frenzy of activity. He imported the finest architects and craftsmen to build the world's greatest monument to love—a magnificent mausoleum that would house the treasured remains of his wife. More than twenty thousand workers took twenty-two years to build it at a cost of billions in today's dollars. Centuries later, it remains one of the architectural marvels of history. It has been dubbed the eighth wonder of the world. When the building was finished, the shah ordered the architectural plans destroyed, the architects murdered, and the hands of the master craftsmen cut off so that their genius could never create anything to rival his magnificent memorial to his wife.

Perhaps you have seen the monument that Shah Jahan erected to his wife, Mumtaz Mahal: the breathtakingly beautiful Taj Mahal. The wife of a British officer was heard to say, "I would gladly die tomorrow if some man loved me enough to put such a building over my grave." An Indian poet wrote of the Taj Mahal, "Only let this one tear-drop, this Tajmahal, glisten spotlessly bright on the cheek of time, forever and ever."

But do you know the little secret that will never appear in a tourist guidebook? Indian researchers have discovered that the ornate burial box does not contain the ashes of Mumtaz Mahal. She is thought to be buried somewhere else, in an unmarked grave. How did this happen? Did Shah Jahan know the awful truth? There are plenty of theories. One is that when Shah Jahan visited the work site, he tripped over a box that had been carelessly left among the rubble. He angrily ordered it to be thrown away. Terrified workers tossed it into a nearby garbage pile where it disappeared forever. But that story is impossible to confirm.

But this much is true: the eighth wonder of the world

perpetrates one of history's greatest frauds. It stands as mute testimony to the tragedy of wasted endeavors. It also raises a question: Are we building magnificent facades that hide empty boxes? One day we will stand before God and give an account for how we have invested his resources. It's good to reflect on an old Italian proverb:

*When the game is over, both king and pawns go back into the same box.*

---

We must all appear before the judgment
seat of Christ, so that each of us may receive
what is due us for the things done while
in the body, whether good or bad.

2 CORINTHIANS 5:10

# Failing Forward

ౚఴఄౚఴ

The only thing that Harland had ever succeeded at was failure. He was just five when his daddy died, leaving his family penniless. At age fourteen, he dropped out of school and hit the road. He worked as a farmhand but soon quit. He became a streetcar conductor but was fired. At age sixteen he lied about his age and joined the army. It wasn't long before he was drummed out of the service. He headed to Alabama, where he tried his hand as a blacksmith. He failed at that, too.

After an unbroken string of failures, Harland found his calling as a locomotive fireman. He figured that he had finally found himself. He was on top of the world when he fell in love and got married. She announced that she was pregnant the day he came home to tell her he had been fired again. A few weeks later, his young wife gave away all their possessions and moved back in with her parents.

Then came the Great Depression. Harland couldn't win for losing. After studying law by correspondence, he was licensed to practice. But he lost his career when he got in a fistfight with one of his clients in a courtroom. He got a gig as a ferryboat captain but was fired after several accidents. He managed a gas station but lost that job when he shot a competitor in an argument over signs.

Later in life he became the chief cook and bottle washer in a little restaurant in Corbin, Kentucky. His establishment became so popular that it put the town on the map, earning him a prestigious award from the governor. Harland was finally a winner. But the new highway bypassed the town, and Harland had to sell his eatery for a fraction of its value. At age sixty-five he was back to square one.

Not long afterward, the mail carrier delivered his first Social Security payment. When he looked at that $105 check, something inside him exploded. He had struggled all his life and had nothing to show for it. So he took that check to the bank and began a fund to start a new venture. That franchise would become one of the most successful in US history.

The man who didn't succeed until he had logged a lifetime of failures, who didn't get started until it was time to stop, was Harland Sanders. You remember him by the title the Kentucky governor gave him: colonel—Colonel Harland Sanders. The business he started with a $105 Social Security check and a "finger lickin' good" recipe was Kentucky Fried Chicken. That little venture that Harland started late in life has become a global empire of 20,000 stores in 125 countries, generating an annual revenue of $23 billion.

Colonel Sanders's story teaches us that it's never too late

to succeed. On the other hand, it's always too soon to give up. No situation is beyond hope. No sin is beyond redemption. No failure is final. Maybe you are on the verge of giving in or giving up. If so, look again at seventy-year-old Harland. He would agree with this:

*Failure is never final or fatal, as long as you fail forward.*

---

The godly may trip seven times, but they will get up again. But one disaster is enough to overthrow the wicked.

PROVERBS 24:16

# Symphonies and Pyramids

cococo

He was a superstar long before the age of superstars. At age five, he wrote a concerto for the harpsichord. Before he was ten, he was composing and publishing violin sonatas. At twelve, he produced his first opera. When he was thirteen, he was the concertmaster of Europe's greatest symphony orchestra. By the time he died of exhaustion, this manic overachiever wrote numerous operettas, cantatas, hymns, oratorios, and arias. He composed forty-eight symphonies and a dozen operas. In his brief life, he gave birth to six hundred compositions!

His music was sheer perfection. His genius has never been matched. This whiz kid with the moniker Johannes Chrysostomus Wolfgangus Theophilus Mozart certainly had a lot of name to live up to.

But there was a dark side to the boy genius. In the 1700s he was living the destructive lifestyle of a modern rock superstar. He was only thirty-five when he collapsed from pneumonia. His drug-addicted wife was in such a stupor that she barely knew her husband had died. A handful of people went to his funeral, but a snowstorm prevented them from going to the grave site. By the time the weather cleared, the grave diggers could not remember where they had buried him. The grave of history's greatest musical genius has never been found.

Compare Mozart's unmarked grave to the most spectacular shrine ever built for a single person. Towering above desert sands outside Cairo, Egypt, it is the most visited grave site in the world. Over one hundred thousand slaves labored and died building the Great Pyramid. Its construction almost bankrupted a nation. After more than four thousand years this grave still stands in crumbling grandeur, although robbers long ago stole the body and plundered the buried wealth. Only a few history buffs remember the name of its original occupant: Pharaoh Khufu. Other than a grave that has become a popular tourist destination, Khufu has left no lasting legacy.

On the other hand, Mozart doesn't even have a weathered stone to mark the fact that he was here. Yet turn the lights in your den down low, slip a CD into the slot, close your eyes, and listen to the exquisite beauty of a Mozart sonata. Race along the highway with the convertible top down, and let the wind rush through your hair as a Mozart symphony blasts gloriously from the speakers. Attend his greatest opera and allow *The Marriage of Figaro* to inflame your senses with soaring passion. Although his body has long ago decomposed in that unmarked grave, his genius lives on forever. One thing is sure: if you look through your CD collection, you won't find anything by an Egyptian pharaoh named Khufu.

It matters little where any of us are buried. It does matter what we compose while still alive on this earth. Every time we love, touch, rescue, or encourage others, they become the living notes of a beautiful symphony that we are composing for the ages. It may not have the perfection of Mozart's musical genius, but our life symphonies will bring joy and beauty long after we are gone. So live today with this in mind:

*Everything will perish, and this world will pass, but the symphony you compose will last forever.*

⁂

Three things will last forever—faith, hope, and love—and the greatest of these is love.

1 CORINTHIANS 13:13

# The Boy They Called Scarface

From the time he was a child, Francis Albert felt that the world was against him. When his mother went into sudden labor, he refused to be born. A doctor used forceps to yank him out, and that violent process tore open the left side of his face and ear. He was deposited in a kitchen sink while the doctor labored to save his mom's life. An aunt finally dunked the baby's lifeless body in cold water. Everyone was stunned when he screamed.

Years later, Francis bitterly confided to a lover, "They ripped me out and tossed me aside to die." Mostly he hated the scars left by the forceps. Later, he suffered more disfigurement from a botched mastoid operation. As a teen, his face was further scarred by cystic acne. He never got over the shame of his classmates calling him Scarface.

His stage mother forced him to enter talent shows, determined that his golden voice would lift his family out of poverty. Francis resented the fact that he could never do enough to please her. After kicking around as a small-time vocalist, he became the lead singer for the Tommy Dorsey Band.

Years before the Beatles, his crooning caused teenage girls to scream and faint.

During World War II, Francis tried to join the army but was rejected as emotionally unfit. It was widely thought that he used his celebrity to shirk his duty.

Columnist Walter Winchell reported that Americans hated Francis more than Hitler. Yet he landed a starring role in an epic war movie and won an Oscar. It was rumored that Francis got his part because a Mafia boss made the director an offer he couldn't refuse. Senator Joseph McCarthy called him a Communist. J. Edgar Hoover was convinced that he had ties to organized crime. Francis felt like the whole world was conspiring against him.

But his star rose in Las Vegas, and John F. Kennedy began to court him. Francis worked tirelessly to get the senator elected US president, only to feel the familiar sting of rejection when the Kennedy family decided Francis was politically toxic. He never recovered from the way he was tossed aside.

You remember Francis by his stage name, Frank. Ol' Blue Eyes made the whole world sing, but his personal life was tragic. He lived in fear of disappointing others and yet trusted no one. He was so embarrassed by his scars that he caked his face in Max Factor makeup. One of his wives said that he took twelve showers a day and constantly changed his clothes and makeup. He obsessed about people who had betrayed him. He alienated his kids and plowed through four marriages.

Daughter Nancy said, "Too bad my dad lived so much of his life before they came up with Zoloft." Francis was a control freak who carefully managed relationships to avoid being hurt again. His biggest hit summed up his life: "I Did It My Way." Those who knew Frank Sinatra best said that he died a lonely man, enslaved to a lifetime of resentments. His sad story sings a final warning:

***When you try to control everything, you end up enjoying nothing.***

⋯⋯⋯

There is no fear in love, but perfect love casts
out fear. For fear has to do with punishment, and
whoever fears has not been perfected in love.

1 JOHN 4:18, ESV

# Straw Dogs

◈

An unpopular war in Vietnam polarized America in 1971. College campuses were rocked by demonstrations. Hippies and pacifists flashed peace signs, but there was no peace. During that turbulence, Hollywood legend Sam Peckinpah gave the nation a deeply disturbing movie. *Straw Dogs* was so brutal that forty years later it was still banned in the United Kingdom. It created a firestorm of controversy in America. That's exactly what Peckinpah wanted.

*Straw Dogs* is about an American college professor, Dr. David Summers, who runs away from the violence in his land. He moves with his British wife, Amy, to an old farmhouse in the English countryside. Summers is a pacifist who will go to any length to avoid confrontation. His unfulfilled wife abhors his weakness.

The professor hires several lads from the local pub to fix the roof on the farmhouse. Ignored by a husband hiding in his study, Amy prances around half naked, flirting shamelessly while the roofers drag out their repair job. David knows they are taking advantage of him but refuses to confront them. He sees the growing magnetism between his wife and one of the lads but retreats into the safe world of complex math equations. The bullyboys laugh behind his back, and Amy despises him all the more.

Emboldened by Amy's flirting and David's passivity, the lads slaughter a cat, hang it in her closet, and then giggle while Amy screams hysterically. They lure David away while one of them rapes his wife. Amy keeps her rape a secret, yet seethes in bitterness when her husband ignores her bruises and tears.

Events spin out of control. The village boys come in the dark of night to finish off the couple. The professor knows that his pacifism will not survive a night of terror. He somehow discovers his courage. While his wife cowers, he frantically runs from room to room trying to lock doors and board up windows. But there are too many openings. Someone breaks through the attic. Others come up through the cellar. David desperately fires a shotgun at one and swings an ax at another. Gore and carnage are everywhere, but he fights on in a frenzy until all the attackers have fled or been killed. Exhausted and covered with blood, the former pacifist whispers, "I will not allow violence against this house."

Sam Peckinpah posed hard questions to an America wrestling with Vietnam. Can pacifism stand in the face of evil? Will wickedness go away if ignored? If war isn't waged against evil when it is small, will we face an inescapable fight to the death when it grows into a monster? *Straw Dogs* is an allegory of spiritual warfare. We flirt with evil, thinking that we can charm the snake. Like Amy, we are caught by surprise when our pet becomes a predator. Or, like the professor, we passively sit by and allow evil to worm its way into our homes and seduce our loved ones. We shouldn't forget the story of a professor and his wife. They would probably agree with this truth:

*The only way for evil to triumph is for good people to do nothing.*

―――― ⌒⌒ ――――

Look, I have given you authority over all the power of the enemy, and you can walk among snakes and scorpions and crush them. Nothing will injure you.

LUKE 10:19

# The Power of Story

༄༅

If the story wasn't true, you might think it to be a fairy tale. An ancient slave people were under a spell that caused them to forget they were once Children of the Light. When these slaves began to outnumber their masters, a wicked king feared that they might seize his dark realm. So he ordered the slaughter of their baby boys. As dragons of death stalked the dark land, a slave woman hid her newborn son in a basket on a river crawling with baby-eating monsters.

Fire angels watched over that baby, and a princess found him in the river. Though she was the daughter of the wicked king, she was kind and brave. She named him Delivered from Water and adopted him as her little prince. He grew up to be a mighty warrior, and he gained the admiration of the evil king. He led the armies of the dark realm to great victories. Delivered from Water had forgotten that he was a son of the enslaved Children of the Light.

Then one day this adopted prince of the dark realm saw an overseer beating a slave. The evil spell was broken, and he knew that he, too, was a Child of the Light. In anger, he slew the slave master. But darkness prevailed, and he had to flee to the desert.

For forty long years the prince wandered as a herder of sheep. He was eighty years old when the Light appeared as a mysterious fire in a twisted bush on a desert mountain. The Light told the shepherd that it was now time for him to free his people. "I can't do it!" protested the shepherd. "I'm not qualified—please send someone else."

The Light responded, "But I will be with you." He gave the old shepherd the supernatural power to turn a stick into a snake. "This is only the beginning of what I will do through you!" he promised. Then he sent him back to the dark realm to confront the evil king and set free the enslaved Children of the Light.

By now you are thinking that this is no fairy tale but a story from Sunday school. It appears in the Jewish Torah and the pages of the Christian Old Testament. It is the true story of Moses, whose name literally means "delivered from water." The delivered one went on to deliver God's people. All fairy tales—and every other story, including yours—are really reflections of a redemptive narrative that makes up the greatest story ever told. God has written your story too. Your personal history is really *his* story. Yours is very special and indispensable to *his* bigger story because *he* took the time to write it just for you. So go out and live another chapter, always remembering this:

*No one loves a good story more than God. That's why he wrote yours.*

———— ᥳᥲᥩᥱᥣ ————

You saw me before I was born. Every day
of my life was recorded in your book. Every
moment was laid out before a single day had
passed. How precious are your thoughts about
me, O God. They cannot be numbered!

PSALM 139:16-17

# "Viva Cristo Rey!"

cᴏᴏ̃ᴏ̃ᴏᴠ

Hidden on a small island off the coast of Cuba is a prison so remote that the outside world didn't know it existed. After the Communist takeover of Cuba in 1959, thousands of Fidel Castro's enemies disappeared in the dark of night. Most were transported to this sinister place called Isla de Pinos—the Isle of the Pines. Among them was a twenty-three-year-old human rights activist, Armando Valladares. He had been sentenced to thirty years at hard labor. What was the crime that earned such a severe prison term? He refused to put a pro-Castro sign on his desk at work. He had been offered a lighter sentence if he would toe the Communist Party line, but he would not.

Valladares later wrote, "For me, it meant 8,000 days of hunger, of systematic beatings, of hard labor, of solitary confinement and solitude, 8,000 days of struggling to prove I was a human being . . . 8,000 days of testing my religious convictions, my faith, of fighting the hate my atheistic jailors were trying to instill in me with every bayonet thrust."

Daily, he watched prisoners being dragged before firing squads. Many were pastors and priests. Just before they were shot, they shouted, "Viva Cristo Rey!"—"Long live Christ the King!" An explosion of gunfire would be followed by deathly quiet. Inmates shouting back from their cells would break the silence: "Viva Cristo Rey!" Eventually the condemned were gagged prior to their execution lest their triumph in the face of death inspire the rest of the prisoners.

Though most of the Christians were Catholics like Valladares, he remembers a Protestant prisoner called the Brother of the Faith. Though repeatedly beaten, he sang hymns at the top of his lungs and shouted to fellow Christians to follow Christ to the end—especially as they were being led to the place of execution.

Valladares writes about the night that prisoners were hauled from their cells to a courtyard where guards began to beat them with rubber hoses and chains. A skeletal figure with long white hair and blazing eyes opened his arms and cried out, "Forgive them, Lord, for they know not what they do." Before he could finish, a lieutenant took quick aim and killed the Brother of the Faith.

Armando Valladares never forgot that martyr or other Christians who were light and salt in the human decay of that prison. After years of suffering the grossest of inhumanities, he was released from the Isla de Pinos. Somehow he made it to the United States and freedom. You can read his story in his book *Against All Hope*. There is a wonderful irony in the title of his book. Hope is the one thing we can never lose, no matter how much is against it.

People can live about thirty days without food, five days without water, and five minutes without air. But they can't live one second without hope. Valladares, the Brother of the Faith, and that company of Cuban martyrs never lost hope as long as they could shout, "Viva Cristo Rey!" Are you going through a tough spell right now? It might help to grab hold of Armando Valladares's story and this hope:

*All the world is full of suffering. It is also full of overcoming.*

⁓

And so, Lord, where do I put my
hope? My only hope is in you.

PSALM 39:7

# The Quadriplegic Ironman

೮ಿ಄಄಄

Ricky was born with the worst kind of cerebral palsy. Doctors said he would be a vegetable for life and recommended that his parents institutionalize him. But his brothers, Rob and Russell, were defiant: "We're going to bring our little brother home and treat him like a regular kid."

Ricky's mom, Judy, refused to surrender to her baby's disability. She spent endless hours doing physical therapy with Ricky, painstakingly taught him the alphabet, and then got state laws changed so that he could attend public school. A special computer allowed him to communicate using head motions to select letters and spell out words.

When he was fifteen years old, Ricky asked his dad if he could compete in a race. His dad agreed, and he pushed his son in a jerry-rigged chair that now resides in the Massachusetts Sports Hall of Fame. After the race, Ricky tapped out a message: "Today I felt like I wasn't handicapped." That started an odyssey that has taken him around the world, averaging fifty races a year, including thirty-four Boston Marathons and a nearly four-thousand-mile bike ride across America.

But it was at the Ironman triathlon in Kona, Hawaii, that a worldwide television audience witnessed Ricky's miracle. Only elite athletes are allowed to compete in this ultra-triathlon of swimming, biking, and running. Ricky and his dad are the only tandem team ever allowed to compete. They came in close to last, but they were the big story in 1997.

The world watched fifty-nine-year-old retired air force colonel Dick Hoyt carry his mute, quadriplegic twenty-seven-year-old son into the Pacific. He swam 2.5 miles in open water, pulling Ricky in a rubber raft attached to his wet suit. After that, he completed the grueling 112-mile bicycle course with Ricky strapped to a seat on his handlebars. Finally, he ran the 26.2-mile marathon while pushing Ricky in a race chair. There have been few moments in sports as inspiring as when Team Hoyt crossed the finish line, Ricky's face grinning with unrestrained joy.

Today Rick Hoyt is a graduate of Boston University. With the help of his caregivers, he lives in an apartment where he develops computers to aid disabled people. Not long ago, he tapped out on his computer to a *Boston Globe* reporter, "When I am running, my disabilities disappear." The reporter said to his dad, "But don't you do the running for your son?" Dick replied, "No, Rick runs the races. I just loan him my arms and legs." He added, "There's nothing in the world that we can't do together."

The story of Team Hoyt should encourage us all. God has

called us to run the race of life. Sometimes it seems beyond our abilities. But we have a heavenly Father who says, "If you do the running, I will give you my arms and legs. There's nothing that we can't do together." So keep on running, inspired by this truth:

*Where our strength runs out, God's strength begins.*

❧

Those who trust in the LORD will find new
strength. They will soar high on wings
like eagles. They will run and not grow
weary. They will walk and not faint.

ISAIAH 40:31

# The Exorcism of a Saint

ᢣᢀᢙᢤ

The old woman had lost her mind. At eighty-six years of age, she took a bad fall and broke her collarbone. Emaciated and frail, she also suffered from heart failure. So she was rushed to a hospital. During the day she curled up in a ball of silent despair. At night she screamed, ripped out her hair, and pulled wires from the monitoring equipment. Nothing could calm her high anxiety.

The archbishop was called to the old woman's room. He couldn't believe that this beloved and saintly woman was contorted in such convulsions of anger. He was sure that she must be demon possessed. So he called a priest to do an exorcism. When the priest saw who she was, he refused.

The archbishop insisted. "I command you to do it!" So he reluctantly obeyed his superior. The woman writhed and screamed while he performed his exorcism. When it was over, she fell into a deep sleep of utter peace.

Who would have guessed that an exorcism would need to be performed on a nun who had earned the Nobel Prize seventeen years earlier? For eighteen years she topped a Gallup Poll as the world's most admired woman. The people of India voted her the most beloved figure in their history. Years after her exorcism, she was canonized as a saint of the Roman Catholic Church.

Now you understand why someone as exalted as the archbishop was called to her room and why a priest hesitated to obey orders to perform an exorcism. Who would believe that Mother Teresa of Calcutta could be demonized? When reports of her exorcism were leaked to CNN, the world was shocked. How could a saint be under such attack by demons? Actually, it makes a lot of sense. Her closest friend, Sister Nirmala, told CNN, "Mother Teresa often felt abandoned by God. But then, Jesus also felt abandoned on the cross."

Most of us have never come remotely close to exhausting ourselves in works of mercy the way Mother Teresa did for more than sixty years. If we did, we might find ourselves suffering with the kind of compassion fatigue that erodes the human soul. We might even find ourselves saying with Jesus, "My God, my God, why have you forsaken me?" (Matthew 27:46, ESV). If we really were a clear and present danger to the kingdom of darkness, we might find ourselves under the most severe kinds of demonic attack. Father Stroscio—who performed Mother Teresa's exorcism—said, "In the history of the church, hundreds of saints have gone through such things."

It is a risky thing to bring the love of Christ to places of suffering and despair. If you have committed to being light and salt where decay and darkness are at their worst, may your tribe increase! You might never be canonized like Mother Teresa, but you are one of those saints who puts a smile on God's face. When the enemy of your soul launches a frontal attack, don't let it fill you with doubt. It goes with the territory. Like Mother Teresa, you will overcome the darkness if you remember this:

*The one who tries to bring you down is already below you.*

❧

Humble yourselves before God. Resist
the devil, and he will flee from you.

JAMES 4:7

# Lieutenant Butch and Easy Eddie

⊷ↂ⊶

T he two men couldn't have been more different. Butch was a World War II fighter pilot who served aboard the USS *Lexington* in the South Pacific. His squadron was on a mission when he radioed that he was leaking fuel. He was ordered to return immediately to his aircraft carrier.

Reluctantly, Butch broke formation and headed back to the fleet. As he burst through the clouds, his blood ran cold. A squadron of Japanese bombers was headed straight for the *Lexington*. Lieutenant Butch O'Hare dove straight into the Japanese formation, his wing-mounted .50-caliber guns blazing. With single-minded focus, he fired until his ammo was spent. Butch then began to ram enemy planes, scattering the bewildered Japanese.

After Butch limped back to the carrier, the camera mounted on his plane showed that he had shot down five Japanese bombers. He was the first naval ace in World War II, and the first naval aviator to win the Congressional Medal of Honor. A year later, Butch O'Hare died in aerial combat at age twenty-nine.

There was another man about the same age as Butch. But Easy Eddie was no hero. This crooked lawyer represented Al Capone, manipulating the legal system to keep the mobster out of prison. Big Al made Eddie the highest-paid attorney in America. His estate was so big that it covered an entire Chicago city block. But Easy Eddie couldn't sleep at night, knowing that he had prostituted himself to the bloodiest mob in gangland history.

Most of all Eddie worried about the legacy he would leave his son. He loved that boy more than life itself, and he wanted him to grow up a better man than he was. But as long as he was associated with Scarface Al Capone, he could never pass on to his son the two most important legacies of all: a good name and a great example. To do that he would have to rectify the crimes he had committed. So he made a courageous decision to walk away from the rackets and testify against Big Al. A year later, Easy Eddie was brutally gunned down by gangsters in Chicago.

The disgraced attorney redeemed a tarnished family name with his final act of heroism. His son grew up proud of the example set by his father, Eddie O'Hare. Maybe it was Eddie's final act of courage that inspired his son Butch to charge that Japanese squadron on February 20, 1942, and later die a hero's death in aerial combat. The next time you fly into Chicago, you might land at O'Hare International Airport, named in honor of Easy Eddie's war-hero son, Lieutenant Commander Butch O'Hare.

Eddie was no saint. Few of us are. But like Easy Eddie, we can work to give our children a good name and a great example. Our sons or daughters may not get an international airport named after them, but we can make it our aim to help them be better than we are. The stories of Easy Eddie and his son, Butch, teach us a great truth:

*Our story is the longest-lasting legacy we will leave to our heirs.*

⸻

The love of the LORD remains forever
with those who fear him. His salvation
extends to the children's children.

PSALM 103:17

# Saving Milly

ccoolo

Most folks didn't think that Mort and Millicent's marriage would go the distance. Mort was a moderate Republican. Millicent was a fiery left-wing Democrat. Over the years, they began to drift in their marriage. It wasn't that they fell out of love. They were just too busy pursuing careers.

Millicent became a psychotherapist working with patients suffering from neurological disorders such as Parkinson's disease. That's how she knew something was wrong that day in 1987. She was signing a check and couldn't finish her name. She noticed a tremor in her little finger and a wobble in her left foot. Millicent was terrified. After tests were run, the news was devastating. Not only did she have Parkinson's disease, it was the most virulent strain.

She called Mort and told him to get home right away. He found her holding a bottle in her trembling hand. "This is Parkinson's medicine!" she screamed. "It's a horrible disease. I won't be able to walk. I won't be able to talk. I won't be able to eat. I'll be totally dependent on you." Her body racked with sobs. "You won't love me anymore. I know that you will leave me."

"I will never leave you," replied Mort. But Millicent wasn't convinced. She knew the statistics. More than 50 percent of husbands leave wives diagnosed with Parkinson's, and she was sure Mort would do the same. At that moment, he had to make a life-altering decision. He knew that Parkinson's victims became completely dependent on their families. If he became a caregiver to his wife, it would derail his career.

You may recall Morton Kondracke, who was the cohost of Fox News channel's *The Beltway Boys*. His rise in the media had been meteoric: ten years as a panelist on the PBS news program *The McLaughlin Group*, senior editor of the *New Republic*, Washington bureau chief of *Newsweek*, columnist for the *Wall Street Journal* and the *Washington Post*, and the most sought-after talking head on prime-time television.

In his book *Saving Milly*, Morton Kondracke wrote, "At that moment I made the decision to change from careerist to a caregiver." For seventeen years he devoted himself to caring for his wife. Eventually Milly was unable to walk or talk, and finally she was unable to swallow. Mort had to feed her, bathe her, and clean up her messes. Mort desperately prayed for Milly. As he spent less time in the newsroom and more in Milly's bedroom, he cried out to God, "What's my purpose here?" A simple answer came back: "Take care of Milly."

When Milly died on July 22, 2004, Mort's career was finished. He had been out of the game too long. But he would tell you that those years he gave to Milly were worth far more.

Careers pale in significance to the care we give loved ones. If you put your life on hold to do what Mort did for Milly, let this encourage you during those often exasperating and thankless hours:

*Careers will fade in importance and soon be forgotten, but heaven's applause for caregivers will last forever.*

⁓

The Son of Man is going to come in his Father's glory with his angels, and then he will reward each person according to what they have done.

MATTHEW 16:27, NIV

# The Man Who Died
# Three Times

୧୬୬୦

Pastor Laszlo Tokes died three times. First he died to his dreams. He left a prestigious pulpit in his native Hungary when he felt God's call to a struggling church among despised minorities in Timisoara, Romania.

Then he died to his career. The Communist authorities put the squeeze on his bishop to muzzle his preaching. Pastor Tokes refused to compromise, so the bishop ordered him to vacate his tiny apartment in the church. After authorities canceled his ration card, his family survived on handouts from parishioners.

Finally he died to life itself. The secret police were coming to arrest him. Everyone knew that when the dreaded Securitate hauled anyone away, they were never seen again. His friends begged him to go into hiding. He responded with Martin Luther's words, "Here I stand. I can do nothing else. If I die, then I die."

A goon squad came in the dark of night on December 15, 1989. To their surprise, three hundred parishioners surrounded the church with arms locked together in solidarity.

Inspired by their pastor's willingness to die, they were willing to give up their lives too. Word of their standoff with the secret police spread and thousands joined them. The bullies from the Securitate retreated, and a revolution that began with tearing down the Berlin Wall six weeks earlier came to Romania.

Two days later a hundred thousand people stormed Communist headquarters in Timisoara, shouting in unison, "God is alive! Jesus is alive!" Word of the uprising spread to the capital city of Bucharest, and almost a million people marched in the streets shouting, "God is alive! Jesus is alive!"

Dictator Nicolae Ceausescu was hiding in his mansion. This hard-line Communist had ruled the country with sadistic cruelty for twenty-four years. He created the Securitate with the largest network of spies and informants in Eastern Europe. Ceausescu declared Romania to be atheistic, but he demanded to be worshiped like a god. This hypocritical socialist and his scheming wife had systematically looted billions from the nation's treasury while living like capitalist royalty.

Yet a pastor's courage brought them down. As protestors surged through the streets, the army turned on their dictator. On Christmas Day, nine days after the Securitate had come to arrest Laszlo Tokes, a military court tried Nicolae and Elena Ceausescu on the charge of genocide. Within two hours they were convicted and executed. A pastor who died to self changed his country, but the dictator who lived for himself was swept into the dustbin of history.

The story of Laszlo Tokes reflects the sacrificial life of the Christ he served. Before there can be a resurrection, there must be death. This uncommonly brave pastor had to die three times before there was new life in Romania. What do you need to die to for things to change for the better? December 16, 1989, proves that what happened in Jerusalem 1,966 years earlier can happen to us, if only we believe this truth:

*Jesus cannot rise in you until you have died to yourself.*

⸺

My old self has been crucified with Christ. It is no longer I who live, but Christ lives in me.

GALATIANS 2:20

# Only the Lonely

∾⊙⊙∽

As a child, Pyotr Ilyich dreaded rejection. His domineering mother repeatedly warned her insecure child that God would turn his back on Pyotr if he wasn't a good little boy! As hard as he tried, Pyotr was too much of a free spirit to please his stern parents. Despite the fact that he was a musical prodigy, his parents insisted that he train for a safe career in the civil service. When he decided to enroll in the music conservatory, his father refused to forgive him. His parents' rejection would twist his soul and unleash his manic genius.

Within a few years, Pyotr was composing music for the ages. Yet critics declared it too romantic, musicians deemed it shallow, and highbrows dismissed it as sentimental. That chorus of criticism plunged him into despair. But common folk flocked to his concerts, making him a superstar. His king proudly proclaimed him a national treasure. He should have been happy with those accolades, but Pyotr invariably allowed a single criticism to cancel out a thousand compliments. Years of rejection had so shattered his psyche that he was constantly suicidal.

A deep secret caused him his greatest anguish. Pyotr was

a closet homosexual. If the truth ever got out, he would be ruined. So he tried to suppress his feelings by getting married. But his new wife was like his disapproving mother. His marriage ended disastrously. He longed to confess his homosexuality to a priest but feared being ostracized by the church. He surely wasn't going to tell his family.

When a homosexual lover exposed him to the world, he suffered a mental breakdown. A Russian court denounced him as a moral degenerate. Some historians speculate that, unhinged by this final condemnation, he ended his life, possibly by drinking arsenic-laced water.

The world knows Pyotr by his anglicized name, Peter—Peter Tchaikovsky. He is celebrated as the musical genius who wrote such masterpieces as the *Romeo and Juliet* overture, scores for ballets like *Swan Lake*, *The Sleeping Beauty*, and *The Nutcracker*, the stirring *1812 Overture*, soaring symphonies, and the opera *Eugene Onegin*. Who would have guessed that such breathtaking beauty was birthed by such a tortured soul?

Before he died, he penned these heartrending words: "None but the lonely feel my anguish." One of life's mysteries is how loveliness is born of ugliness or greatness is forged out of affliction. God always does his greatest work through the most flawed people. It might help us all to make this our faith credo when, like Peter Tchaikovsky, our story is filled with lonely anguish:

*God can take my pain and use it to turn my life into a masterpiece.*

⌘

Consider it pure joy . . . whenever you face
trials of many kinds, because you know that the
testing of your faith develops perseverance.

JAMES 1:2-3, NIV

# The Miracle at Naseby

❧

Nothing much ever happens in sleepy Naseby. Yet by happenstance of history, two armies collided there on the morning of June 14, 1645. The battle outside that little village would change the course of Western civilization.

Massed on the sheep pasture outside Naseby was the proud army of His Catholic Majesty King Charles I of England. His Royalist forces were shined and polished, their steel and muskets flashing in the cold sunlight under scarlet banners dancing in the breeze. Supporting the massed infantry were the Cavaliers, the finest swordsmen and cavalry in Europe, led by Prince Rupert, the swashbuckling nephew of King Charles. With swaggering bravado, he boasted that his Cavaliers would rout their ragtag enemy and be back in camp in time for lunch.

Across the field, the army of Parliament waited with fear rising in their throats. Mostly made up of drafted farmers and vastly outnumbered, they stood little chance at Naseby that day. While royal princes led the king's forces, Parliament's army was led by rugged Puritans more familiar with Bibles and plows than muskets and cannons. Among them was a farmer, Oliver Cromwell, leading the cavalry that would face Prince Rupert and his Cavaliers that morning.

Cromwell shouted out to his men, "Boys, keep your powder dry and your prayer books handy. Our battle is in the Lord's hands, and he alone gives the victory." As one man, his army fell to their knees. One by one, Puritan preachers among these farm boys began to cry out for supernatural strength.

At Naseby the prayers of country bumpkins overcame the polished steel of the royal army. Prince Rupert and his vaunted Cavaliers charged across the field, only to be outmaneuvered by Cromwell and put to flight. The army of Parliament surged forward and the rout was on. Prince Rupert was right: the battle was over before lunch. But it was the Royalists who were broken and in disarray.

The fate of a civil war that divided England was decided that day. It wasn't long before the rule of elected assembly replaced the absolute authority of the king. On the fields of Naseby, the blood of citizen farmers purchased a radical new government that would later flower in America.

Those of us who enjoy the freedoms of a government of the people, by the people, and for the people, should never forget the moment that turned the tide from king to Parliament that day. As Prince Rupert's Cavaliers charged across the field, Oliver Cromwell whispered a prayer to God before he pulled down the visor of his helmet: "If in the heat of battle this day, I should forget to remember thee, I pray that thou wouldst not forget me." Surely, the Lord did not forget him.

Cromwell's army was at its most lethal when it was on its knees in prayer. A battlefield may be looming before you today. Perhaps the odds are overwhelming. Before you pull down the visor to your helmet and march off to war, why don't you get down on your knees? The battle of Naseby is another proof of this inviolate principle of warfare:

*The greatest powers cannot overcome the humblest prayers.*

───── ✦ ─────

It is not by force nor by strength, but by my Spirit, says the LORD of Heaven's Armies.

ZECHARIAH 4:6

# Let's Hear It for
# the Boll Weevil

⟡⟐⟡

If you've ever been down to Coffee County in Southeastern Alabama, you know that there's not much to see. But it's worth the trip to stop off in the small town of Enterprise. There's not a whole lot to see there, either. But there is one attraction you won't see anywhere else in the world.

In the town square there is a thirteen-foot-high marble statue of a woman standing in splendor atop an ornate base in the middle of a fountain. Her arms stretch up in a pose of worship. This classic sculpture, looking like something you might see in Rome, seems strangely out of place in rural Alabama. But then you see what she holds in her hands as an offering to heaven: a giant, black boll weevil. More astounding are the words inscribed on her base: "In profound appreciation of the Boll Weevil and what it has done as the Herald of Prosperity."

Wait a minute! In profound appreciation of the boll weevil? The boll weevil is a herald of prosperity? Certainly not where there is cotton! And cotton was king for two hundred years in Coffee County. Boll weevils are especially fond of cotton. An infestation of these black devils can strip a cotton field bare in a few days. So why build a statue in "profound appreciation" of these voracious pests?

You have to go back to the late 1800s to answer that question. That's when a plague of boll weevils crossed over from Mexico, eating a destructive swath across the cotton patch of Southeastern America. By the time the insects reached Coffee County, panic was in the air. Cotton was the engine that drove the economy. There wasn't a living soul that didn't depend on cotton. By 1910 boll weevils covered Alabama like a swarming, crawling, devouring black flood. The annual yield of cotton was cut by 40 percent. Statewide revenue losses were more than 70 percent. Farmers lost whole crops. Many had to abandon farms that had been in their families for generations. Historians agree that, other than the Civil War, nothing devastated the South like the boll weevil.

To survive, cotton farmers had to turn to more diversified farming. Most of all they planted peanuts. By 1917, some twenty-four years after the first boll weevils arrived, Coffee County was producing more than one million bushels of peanuts annually. Enterprise had become known as the peanut capital of the world. Coffee County was more prosperous than it had ever been when cotton was king.

In that year of unprecedented prosperity, the grateful citizens of Enterprise erected their shrine to the boll weevil—the only memorial to an insect anywhere in the world. It was dedicated with a prayer of thanksgiving to God for allowing the greatest crisis in their history. Sometimes things have to fall apart before they can fall together. We may have to lose good things so that we can get better things. The folks in Enterprise would say amen to something Coach John Wooden often said:

*Things turn out best for the people who make the best of the way things turn out.*

⁓

So be truly glad. There is wonderful joy
ahead, even though you must endure
many trials for a little while.

1 PETER 1:6

# The Reluctant Spy

❧

Nate lived quietly in the shadows. As the sixth of ten brothers, he was mostly ignored. Frail and sickly, he stayed indoors by the fireplace. While other boys explored frontier forests, he burrowed into books. When his brothers plowed fields alongside their father, he talked poetry with his mother. By age eleven, this bookworm was fluent in Greek, Latin, and Hebrew. No one was surprised when he became Yale College's youngest student at age fourteen or when he graduated with top honors when he was only eighteen.

By now, colonial America was a hotbed of revolution. Down south, Patrick Henry electrified Virginia's House of Burgesses with his immortal words "Give me liberty or give me death!" But Nate was a gentle and meek scholar. Some even whispered that he was fainthearted or maybe cowardly. While other young men were taking up arms, this teacher retreated to the safety of his classroom.

Then came the British siege of Boston. Embarrassed to be thought a coward, he joined the local militia. Yet when his students marched off to war, Nate stayed behind. While they shed their blood on the battlefield, he hid in his classroom.

But a sentence in a letter from a Yale classmate gnawed at him: "Our holy religion and the honor of God demand that we defend our country." That single line put steel in the frail bookworm's spine.

Soon after, he joined George Washington's army. When they made him a supply officer, he was relieved that his duties kept him far from battle. But a line in another letter jabbed at his conscience: "Now is the time for great men to immortalize their names in the defense of their country." When Washington needed a volunteer to spy out British troop strength on Long Island, Nate surprised everyone by impulsively stepping forward.

Never was a spy more fearful. Maybe that's why he was spotted within hours of landing in Manhattan. He was arrested and dragged before British general William Howe. He was summarily condemned as a spy, sentenced to death, and locked in a greenhouse for the night. We might wish that Nate faced his death with dignity. Instead, he shook with fear and vomited repeatedly. He asked for a Bible, but it was refused. At dawn he begged for a chaplain, but that, too, was denied. He was marched down the road to a tree by the local tavern. His knees buckled, but his resolve didn't. As the noose was placed around his neck, Nate quoted a line from Joseph Addison's play *Cato*, spoken by the Roman patriot Cato as he is being martyred: "I regret that I have but one life to give for my country."

When Nate's brothers came to reclaim his body, the British had already dumped it in an unmarked grave. Though the body was never recovered, a grateful nation hasn't forgotten Nate or his full name: Nathan Hale. Surely he immortalized his name with sacred honor in the defense of his country. If we wish to pass on to our children the liberties given to us at such great sacrifice, we ought to recall another line from *Cato*. Surely Nate had read these words too:

*He who fears death has already lost the life he covets.*

⚬⚬⚬

Greater love has no one than this: to lay
down one's life for one's friends.

JOHN 15:13, NIV

# A Message in a Bottle

୧୭୭୭

In 1972 *Voyager 2* was launched. Its projected journey was 1.4 billion miles. It passed Jupiter in 1979. Traveling at speeds of thirty-five thousand miles per hour, it hurtled past Saturn, Uranus, and Pluto before plunging into interstellar space in 1990.

Aboard the *Voyager 2* is a recording of the sounds of Earth. Babies crying and children laughing. Traffic jams and jackhammers. Singing of choirs, music of symphonies, and songs of romance. The pulsating beat of heavy metal rock music. The screams of airplanes and the fury of nature. A cacophony of sounds that capture the essence of life on this planet.

Those sounds serve as a time capsule, waiting for someone to make it play. Today, out in the distant vastness of the universe, a lonely spacecraft journeys toward an unknown destination, ready to break the silence of outer space with the sounds of humanity.

It has a surrealistic feel to it. Did the scientists at NASA put a message in a bottle and cast it into a cosmic ocean? Did they fear that we stand on the precipice of a nuclear, biological, or ecological holocaust? Were they afraid that our geopolitical house of cards might collapse into apocalyptic chaos?

Maybe *Voyager 2* is a cry for help from a distressed planet. A high-tech toss of the dice that some superior intelligence out there might hear the sounds of Earth. Like a bottle placed in the sea by a marooned sailor, *Voyager 2* bobs through the trackless reaches of the cosmic ocean with a recorded message: "If you are out there, this is Earth. If there is still time, help us. If our time has run out, remember us."

But there's good news for the programmers of *Voyager 2*, or for anyone else who has lost hope. There is someone out there, beyond the farthest expanse of our cosmic ocean. He knows that we exist. He never misses a single sound, especially our cries for help.

He didn't wait for us to perfect our technology so we could toss a bottle with a message into the interstellar seas. Two thousand years ago, he left heaven to come to a lost and dying planet. He humbled himself to enter the womb of an unwed teenage girl. From the moment of conception, this baby was fully God and fully human. His earthly name was Jesus. He was born to die so that he might redeem this Earth and all those who receive him as Savior and Lord. He rose from the dead and went back to heaven. But he's coming again to make everything right. Remember, history is *his* story. He writes it with a happy ending for those who belong to him.

As you consider your own salvation, think about the haunting story of *Voyager 2* and the happier story of heaven's great rescue operation that was launched just for you. Maybe this new take on something Saint Augustine said will resonate with your heart:

**God has made us for himself, and his heart will be restless until we find our rest in his arms.**

⸙

This is real love—not that we loved God,
but that he loved us and sent his Son as
a sacrifice to take away our sins.

1 JOHN 4:10

# Unbroken by Failure

ᘓᗐᕮᗑᕬ

He was seven years old when his family lost their Indiana farm. He had to drop out of school and go to work. Two years later his beloved mother died. When he was twenty-two years old he started a business. Within a year, it went belly up. He ran for the state legislature and lost. Someone hired him to run a store but fired him a few months later. So he applied to law school only to be rejected. A friend loaned him money to start another business. Within a year, he filed for bankruptcy. It took him seventeen years to pay off his debt.

Again he made a run at politics. He finally got a rare taste of success. The year he took office, he got engaged. It seemed that fortune was finally smiling on him. But on the eve of their wedding, his fiancée died of typhoid fever, and he plunged into suicidal despair. He spent the next six months in bed.

He recovered enough to get back into the political game but was defeated. His friends tried to cheer him up by pushing him into an arranged marriage. It would be the great disaster of his life, consigning him to twenty-three years with a difficult wife.

Again he ran for public office, suffering yet another defeat. Then his three-year-old son Edward died. After a season of grief, he finally won an election, only to lose his bid for reelection. When he limped home from Washington, DC, he ran for some minor office in his home state, only to be rejected again.

After licking his wounds for five years, he ran for the US Senate and lost. Sympathetic colleagues nominated him for vice president. He finished dead last among all the candidates. Two years later, he picked himself off the floor and ran for the senate a second time. Again he was defeated, giving him the dubious distinction of being the biggest political loser in US history.

It's a miracle that two years later he somehow found the courage to run for America's highest office. In 1860, after decades of political failures and personal setbacks, Abraham Lincoln became the sixteenth president of the United States.

But his euphoria was short lived. As the country careened toward civil war, he was vilified across the South. Newspapers lampooned him, calling him the Gorilla from Illinois. When the Union dissolved, there were calls for the president's impeachment. His generals refused his orders, and cabinet members plotted against him. His eleven-year-old son died, and his wife descended into madness. In the end, he was denied the pleasure of savoring his greatest triumph when he was assassinated only six days after the Civil War ended.

As he stood by Lincoln's deathbed, the secretary of state whispered, "He now belongs to the ages." Two days later, on Good Friday, preachers across America eulogized Lincoln as the savior of our nation. If you have gone through a long stretch of defeats and are ready to throw in the towel, you might want to remember Abraham Lincoln's story in the light of something Leo Tolstoy wrote:

***The two most powerful warriors are patience and time.***

⁓

Wait patiently for the LORD. Be brave and courageous. Yes, wait patiently for the LORD.

PSALM 27:14

# The Counterfeit Artist

୧୭୨୬

H is neighbors wondered how the recent immigrant always seemed to have so much cash. Some of it was in big bills. His small farm in New Jersey couldn't produce enough to give him that kind of spending money. When they asked the distinguished gentleman, he would demurely reply in a heavy German accent that he was receiving a pension from the Prussian army.

When he entered a small neighborhood grocery store to purchase some turnip greens, he handed the clerk a twenty-dollar bill. In 1887 not many people paid with bills that large. It wouldn't be easy to find change for twenty-five cents' worth of greens. Then as the clerk rummaged through her drawer looking for change, she noticed ink on her fingers. She was shocked. The German was a longtime friend. Surely he wouldn't give her a bill that wasn't genuine. The clerk shrugged off her suspicions and handed the man his change.

Later she had second thoughts. Twenty dollars was two weeks' salary in 1887. So she reluctantly summoned the local police. As it turned out, treasury officials had spent eleven years trying to track down the mysterious forger who had been circulating counterfeit bills in the Northeast. Having no clue as to his identity, agents nicknamed him Jim the Penman.

Nine years later, the German tried to pay a bartender with a fifty-dollar note. When the barkeep's wet hands smudged the ink, he called the authorities. Secret Service agents arrested Emanuel Ninger. When they searched his home, they found expensive paper and sophisticated paintbrushes. Ninger had taken weeks meticulously, painstakingly hand painting each bill. He may have created seven hundred counterfeit bills in eighteen years—many works of art, highly valued by collectors today.

Though the public admired him as a Robin Hood figure, the Feds weren't amused. Ninger spent six years in the penitentiary. When he got out, he took a stab at counterfeiting British pound notes. He just couldn't go straight. But his isn't the usual story of crime that doesn't pay. It's much more tragic than that. His is the story of a life and talent wasted.

When the Secret Service agents confiscated his counterfeiting paraphernalia, they also seized three portraits that he had painted. After his arrest, they were sold at public auction for $16,000. That averages out to more than $5,000 a portrait—a fabulous sum in 1896. Ninger later admitted that it took the same amount of time to paint a twenty-dollar bill as it did a $5,000 portrait. Yet when he got out of prison, he went back to counterfeiting! Emanuel Ninger's story of a wasted life begs a question of us all: Are we misusing our energy and talents in pursuit of lesser things when God has made us to create eternal things? Here's a contemporary take on something Sidney J. Harris once said:

*People make counterfeit money; in many more cases, money makes counterfeit people.*

───── ✦ ─────

Don't store up treasures here on earth, where moths eat them and rust destroys them, and where thieves break in and steal. Store your treasures in heaven, where moths and rust cannot destroy, and thieves do not break in and steal.

MATTHEW 6:19-20

# The Dance of Fools

⋘⊙⊙⋙

S he stands aloof, like an eagle perched high above lesser creatures, looking down her haughty beak at the streets below. A celebration has broken out, and the riffraff celebrate with vulgar gusto. But her deepest disgust is in her husband, who has thrown off his royal robes and is dancing like a fool with the household maids.

It wasn't always like this. Once upon a time she was in love with the shepherd who had slain a giant. It was the stuff of fairy tales: the princess and the shepherd. When her daddy, the king, gave her to him in marriage it was headline news: "Royal Marries Commoner." But they did not live happily ever after. When her shepherd grew too popular, her father tried to kill him. She risked her life helping him escape. Lonely weeks turned to long months. When the king forced her to marry a mousy shadow of her shepherd, the princess prayed fervently that her hero would return to rescue her.

But disturbing news filtered back to the palace. Her fugitive first husband was now a Robin Hood, his band of outlaws living off the land while leading the king's men on a merry chase. He also took on new wives. When she heard the devastating news, her passions shriveled, and she walled off her heart until it became as cold as ice.

Then her father and brothers were killed in battle. A civil war erupted between her first husband and her father's royal house. When his rivals were eliminated, the shepherd demanded that she be sent back to him. Yet he reclaimed her not as a returning lover, but as a king taking back stolen property. Her second husband trailed behind, wailing hysterically and further humiliating her.

Weep for Michal, the proud daughter of King Saul. The shepherd once thought himself the luckiest man alive to marry her. Now she is his trophy wife, a political commodity to solidify his reign by connecting it to the old royal house. Weep for dreams dashed and for the bitterness that has robbed Michal of her joy in her king.

The Ark of the Covenant has been returned, bringing the very presence of God into Jerusalem. David has disrobed and is dancing like a mad fool in unbridled joy before his Lord. But when he returns exhausted from his worship, he is met by the ice queen who used to be a princess. She spits out pent-up anger: "How dare you disrobe and dance like a vulgar fellow?" She has forever shut the door to her king. He walks away, never to return to Michal's bedroom again.

A thousand years later, the great Son of David rides through the same gates of Jerusalem. As with the Ark of the Covenant, God's presence is in him. Indeed, Jesus is God in the flesh. The crowds dance like joyous fools before him. Soon this king, too, will disrobe to hang on a cross. High above in the Temple, the icy spirit of Michal lives again in religious leaders. They don't want their king either. So they shut the door to his love. How about you? Don't let Michal's sad story be yours.

*The King has come! Open your heart and join the dance!*

⸙

> You have turned my mourning into joyful dancing. . . . that I might sing praises to you and not be silent.

PSALM 30:11-12

# Latrodectus Mactans

༻☙☙⊶

Her name is *Latrodectus mactans*. The lady is black and beautiful, with an hourglass figure. It's her honeymoon night, and she dances before her husband to arouse his passions. More than anything *Latrodectus* wants babies. When the night of lovemaking is over and she is satisfied that she is pregnant, she gives him a fatal kiss—a dagger plunged into his body. On its point is poison fifteen times more toxic than the venom of a prairie rattlesnake. She then proceeds to eat her husband's body. It is a deliciously ingenious way to dispose of the evidence of her hideous crime.

It's not the first time that *Latrodectus* has committed such a ghastly deed, nor will it be the last. This serial killer waddles away, fat on the remains of her slain husband, to lay up to 750 eggs. She has earned her alias: the black widow. Anyone who has ever been bitten by the spider with the scientific name *Latrodectus mactans* can attest to the severity of her venom.

Forensic experts call women who kill their husbands black widows. Surprisingly, women are guilty of 41 percent of spousal homicides in America. Men most often kill outside their families. But women are far more likely to murder members of their own families—usually husbands. The number one reason is spousal abuse. The second is money.

The most infamous black widow was Belle Gunness. She stood at five-and-a-half feet tall and weighed a hefty 270 pounds. She was a rough farm woman who wore overalls, pitched hay, and butchered hogs. No one would have guessed that Belle was a femme fatale. But when she put on her corset and piled up her hair in the latest style, she became a lethal seductress. After she disappeared in 1908, investigators found more than forty poisoned victims buried on her farm. Before the books were closed, it was determined that Belle murdered forty people, including multiple husbands and all her children.

History crawls with black widows who devour men for their money. Lucy Trueblood poisoned five spouses, a brother-in-law, and her only child. Rhonda Bell Martin killed two husbands, her mother, and three of her children for their insurance. After autopsies revealed the grisly truth, this Alabama black widow was executed in 1957.

We are shocked and horrified at such stories. Yet they might hit close to home, especially if we are religious. Remember that God has always called Israel his bride. When Jesus came, he was the fulfillment of the prophecies that a Savior would come as a husband to rescue his bride. But the "black widow" religious leaders ensnared their husband in a web of deceit, pierced him with poison, and devoured his body. Yet he rose again. He loves us too much to leave us to our sin. So crush the spider and embrace the Savior.

*It wasn't our nails but his love that kept Jesus on that cross.*

━━━━ ⌘ ━━━━

God showed his great love for us by sending
Christ to die for us while we were still sinners.

ROMANS 5:8

# The Prince of Preachers

෴

At twenty-one years of age, he was his nation's biggest celebrity. His Sunday sermons were printed on the front page of newspapers and then reproduced and sold on London streets. The demand for these printed sermons was so great that more than a hundred million copies were sold worldwide. Explorer David Livingston even carried them in his pockets as he hacked his way through African jungles.

So many people wanted to hear him preach that police had to be called in for crowd control. The biggest auditoriums in London weren't big enough. So he announced that he would preach in the music hall at the Royal Surrey Gardens. Polite society was scandalized. Vaudeville shows and circuses performed before raucous, beer-swilling crowds at the Surrey Music Hall.

British clergymen railed against him and newspaper articles condemned him as a publicity-seeking sensationalist. Yet on a Sunday evening in October of 1858, traffic jams stretched back seven miles as massive crowds shoved their way into the Surrey Gardens. As the young pastor stood up before the packed music hall, several people began to yell,

"Fire!" Panicked people stampeded to the exits. Seven people were crushed to death and twenty-eight critically injured. The preacher boy was led out past twisted corpses laid out on the lawn. When he got home, he collapsed into his young wife's arms, sobbing uncontrollably. He was carried to his bed, where he lay in a fetal position for two weeks. In the days to follow, both preachers and newspaper editorials across Great Britain said that the tragedy was God's judgment on holding a church service on the devil's playground.

We can be glad that young Charles Spurgeon finally got up. He overcame suicidal despair to start a college, open a string of orphanages, and produce sixty-four volumes of the greatest sermons ever preached. At age twenty-three he ignored his critics and held services at the Crystal Palace, the largest auditorium in England. He spoke to the biggest crowds ever to hear a preacher. Four years later he opened the mammoth Metropolitan Tabernacle, the first megachurch in history.

Though he has been called the Prince of Preachers and countless millions have been transformed by his ministry, Spurgeon suffered severe depression for the rest of his life. Though his sermons were full of humor, he wrote, "Melancholy is my closest neighbor." There were times when flashbacks of that night in the Surrey Music Hall would come in the middle of a sermon, and he would have to be carried home in a stupor. He would experience seasons of enthusiasm, only to spend other months in bed. Before he died at age fifty-eight, he was revered as the greatest preacher of his age. But he was also morbidly obese and suffering from gout and rheumatism, all complicated by his bouts with depression.

Does it surprise you that such a great hero of the Christian faith should suffer chronic despair? It shouldn't. From the prophet Elijah to Mother Teresa, many of history's greatest saints have struggled with depression. But they have discovered that God's grace is often painted on the canvas of despair. In times of suffering, this truth deserves meditation:

*The unwounded life bears no resemblance to Jesus.*

⁓

I bear on my body the scars that
show I belong to Jesus.

GALATIANS 6:17

# Theo's Big Brother

❦

It was bad enough that Theo's older brother was ravaged in body and sick at heart. Now he was locked in an insane asylum because his neighbors said he was too crazy to be on the loose.

Maybe things would have been different if his preacher father hadn't been so austere or his mother so moody. Theo's older brother never felt loved as a child, nor could he shake the fact that his parents had given him the same name as their stillborn son, who had been delivered exactly one year before he was born. It's hard enough to see your name and birth date etched on a tombstone; it's devastating to feel that you're a replacement for the child your grieving parents really wanted.

He tried to curry favor with his father by studying for seminary and then volunteering to serve at a poor church other preachers avoided. He loved working among poor miners and potato eaters. They returned his love by nicknaming him Christ of the Coal Mines. It was the only time Theo's big brother ever felt loved. But before long, church leaders fired him for being too unconventional.

He tried his hand at art but insisted on painting subjects

no one wanted to see on canvas. He sold only one out of more than two thousand paintings. He searched for romance, even resorting to bizarre acts in the name of love, but he was rejected by every woman except an alcoholic prostitute. It wasn't long before he, too, was drowning in booze.

Now he was in the asylum, looking through bars at a starry night. The world can thank Theo for believing that his older brother still had a spark of genius. If he hadn't brought art supplies to the asylum, perhaps his brother wouldn't have put on canvas what he saw through the bars. The lunatic laid his work aside with a shrug. No one would purchase this painting either.

When he was released, he took the painting to Theo's apartment along with the other unsold canvases full of sunflowers, reapers, and potato eaters. Theo promised to sell the works, but his older brother had already given up hope. Not long after, he shot himself. When Theo took his body to the church, the priest refused to hold a funeral for a man who had committed suicide. Instead, Theo took the coffin to a tavern, surrounded it with his brother's paintings, and celebrated his memory with drunks, starving artists, and prostitutes.

Theo died before he could sell his brother's paintings. But Theo's widow, Johanna van Gogh, made good on her husband's promise to Vincent. She might be shocked to know that one day Vincent van Gogh's *Starry Night*, seen through the bars of that asylum, would become his most famous work—or that one of his paintings would fetch as much as $82 million.

No life is ever wasted or without hope. Even in a hopeless asylum, we can still see a starry night through the bars. Theo's older brother gave up hope too soon. You won't, if you hold on to this truth:

***It takes the darkest nights to produce the brightest stars.***

———— ❧ ————

He counts the stars and calls them all by name.
How great is our Lord! His power is absolute!

PSALM 147:4-5

# Singing to Johnny

ᥫᩍᥬ

Christine was proclaimed one of the outstanding singers in America. She had big offers from record labels and was looking forward to a full schedule of concerts. Her agent predicted that she would be a recording star. Singing was her life and performing was her passion.

Everything changed that harrowing night Christine gave birth to baby Johnny. The doctor was inexcusably drunk. He broke several of the baby's bones as he pulled him from the birth canal. The violence of that delivery resulted in severe hemorrhaging of the newborn's brain. The inebriated obstetrician would lose his license to practice and later commit suicide. But that didn't help Christine's baby.

During the first year, eight doctors said that he could not possibly survive. For his first two years, she had to feed him every three hours with a special feeder. It took more than an hour to accomplish each feeding. During those two years Christine never left her home. She didn't get more than two hours of sleep at any one time. The voice that enraptured thousands now sang simple lullabies to a child with severe disabilities.

Johnny lived twenty-four years. He was totally paralyzed, only able to sit in a wheelchair with the assistance of a full-length body brace. Convinced that God had called her to care for her son, Christine never went back to the concert stage. She bathed, clothed, and lifted his limp body in and out of the wheelchair, spoon-fed him—and above all, sang to him.

Christine's husband, John Edmund Haggai, is a noted evangelist, author, and global missions leader. He wrote her story in his moving book *My Son Johnny*. What amazed him most was the way Christine showered their son with unconditional love for more than eight thousand straight days. She never once resented the fact that her music career died the day Johnny was born. She felt that God had given her a voice to sing her boy into heaven. Even more amazing was the fact that she never complained that she was marooned in a small world with a helpless son who demanded every ounce of her energy and patience.

But the thing that most impressed John Haggai was that he never once heard Christine say an unkind word about the doctor who injured her son and destroyed her career. In fact, she wept when she heard that he had committed suicide. Her forgiveness of that obstetrician was as complete and unconditional as her love for Johnny.

Her husband proudly said that at age forty, after years of unending servitude, Christine possessed the youthful sparkle that would be the envy of any high school senior, and the charm and beauty for which any debutant would gladly give a fortune. Haggai believed that her ability to forgive made her more beautiful. Isn't that what makes Jesus so immeasurably beautiful? Nowhere do you see that more than when Jesus forgave those who crucified him. When we fail to forgive those who have hurt us deeply, or resent circumstances that derail our dreams, we need to remember something that Martin Luther King Jr. often said:

*Forgiveness is not an occasional act but a permanent attitude.*

---

He has removed our sins as far from
us as the east is from the west.

PSALM 103:12

# Decision at Twenty-Nine Thousand Feet

∾⊙⊙∾

They spotted him just after sunrise, perched on a knife-edge ridge. He sat in the brutal cold without jacket, gloves, or hat. Australian climber Lincoln Hall had been left for dead. American guide Dan Mazur, two paying clients, and a Sherpa were just hours from the summit of Mount Everest on May 26, 2006, when they spied Hall.

The American had to react quickly. Would his team continue their assent to the top or help Hall? Mazur decided to help. Two other climbers passed them on their way to the summit. When asked to help, the two pretended not to understand. Mazur later discovered that they spoke impeccable English. Even more astounding was the fact that a week before Hall's rescue, British climber David Sharp died one thousand feet from the top while dozens passed by on their way to the summit. But Mazur's team lugged Lincoln Hall back down, forfeiting their prize.

Before we fault climbers who bypassed Hall and Sharp, we should consider what it costs to get to the summit. The weather on Mount Everest is so brutal that there are only two windows a year for climbing, each about ten days. Fewer than half the climbers succeed in their attempt. Some 280 have died trying.

Climbing Everest isn't cheap, starting at $45,000. It begins with an eight-day hike from Kathmandu to the seventeen-thousand-foot base camp. The entire expedition will take about two months. As they head out from base camp, climbers face soaring ice towers and crevasses so deep that one can only see darkness rather than bottom. It's beautiful, otherworldly, and dangerous. One misstep can lead to death.

Towering waves of ice—several stories high—crack and collapse to create avalanches that bury climbers alive or plunge them into crevasses. At twenty thousand feet the air contains half the oxygen that it does at sea level. The sun radiating off the snow can create temperatures of 80 to 100 degrees Fahrenheit, leading to heat exhaustion, or plunge to 50 degrees below zero, bringing hypothermia. At twenty-two thousand feet, climbers must scale the Lhotse Face, a 3,600-foot wall of ice. At this point they are breathing bottled oxygen. Winds can blow 175 miles per hour, a category five hurricane. At twenty-three thousand feet, climbers are beyond rescue by helicopters.

Above twenty-five thousand feet, climbers enter the death zone. Many suffer swelling of the brain and fluid in the lungs. It's half a mile from high camp to the summit, but the final ascent will take eight to twelve hours. Oxygen is now one-third of what it is at sea level. If climbers make it up Hillary Step for a few moments on a summit about the size of a dining room table, they now face the most lethal part of the trip: descending the twenty-nine-thousand-foot monster. Slowed judgment and reflexes from exhaustion cause mistakes that lead to far more deaths than on the way up.

When Mazur and his team chose to rescue Lincoln Hall, forfeiting their dreams so tantalizingly close to the summit, it was an amazing act of mercy. Showing mercy is often messy, and it is seldom easy. It cost God's Son everything. It will cost us, too. But even if we are twenty-nine thousand feet up, we need to remember this:

*Every breath in your life is a gift of God's mercy.*

———— ⌒⌒ ————

God blesses those who are merciful,
for they will be shown mercy.

MATTHEW 5:7

# Too Big to Miss

⌒⊙⊙⌒

Judean winds whistle through the valley, calling the present to remember the past. As you pick up stones in a dried-up creek bed, through the ears of your imagination you hear the rattling of swords as ancient spirits rise to fight again. Then cars on a nearby freeway jolt you back to reality. You wonder if these passing motorists realize what took place in this Valley of Elah some three thousand years ago. Let your thoughts take you back to that magical day.

A giant lumbers out across that valley day after day. Goliath is the original Megatron, standing some nine feet tall. With his enormous bulk, armor, and weapons, he weighs in at some six hundred pounds—one gargantuan mass of bronze glistening in the Judean sun. The Philistines have found their weapon of mass destruction in this incredible hulk.

Half the valley shakes as he bellows his blasphemies across the creek in a voice that is Darth Vader on reverb. "Choose a man, and have him come out and fight me!" But the Israelites cower behind rocks, mesmerized, hypnotized, and paralyzed. For forty straight days they watch helplessly as the giant struts his awesome stuff.

Not much has changed in three thousand years. Every day, giants lumber forth to challenge us. We crawl out of bed and march out to battle, banging on shields and rattling sabers. We boast that *this* time we will beat our Goliath. Then the giant roars, and our courage melts.

According to tradition, Goliath had four brothers, all of them giants too. Giants come at us in packs. They appear in various shapes and sizes. Only you know the Goliaths you will face in your Valley of Elah. But God made you to be a giant slayer.

Look again. Do you see the herder of sheep from Bethlehem? He's just a pipsqueak boy. Get to know David, and you discover that he has feet of clay just like you. You may only have a few stones and a sling. Yet ablaze with God's Spirit, pipsqueaks with clay feet topple giants. And when they have the courage to walk out into the valley of giants, the people of God take heart. They rise up with a shout, inspired by a pipsqueak with a slingshot. Those who dare to be a David become the leaders who change the world.

Maybe it's all about perspective. King Saul was a mighty warrior, towering above everyone else in Israel. But Saul was a big man with a small heart. He took one look at Goliath and said, "That giant's too big to hit." David was the runt of the litter, but he had a heart bigger than all outdoors. He looked at Goliath and said, "He's too big to miss." David could have written the German proverb that says, "Fear makes the wolf bigger than he is." Perhaps David looked a thousand years into the future and saw his great descendant Jesus of Nazareth defeat Goliath when he crushed Satan at the Cross. If you are facing some giant today, remember this amazing fact:

*When Jesus defeated Satan, he toppled all our giants too. We simply have to rise up and claim victories already won.*

⁂

Thank God! He gives us victory over sin and death through our Lord Jesus Christ. So, my dear brothers and sisters, be strong and immovable.

1 CORINTHIANS 15:57-58

# Butterfly Miracles

⁓

Cancer had reduced six-year-old Christian to skin and bones. It was during his final days that nature bestowed its annual miracle. Millions of yellow butterflies invade northeast Oklahoma with a gentle firestorm of color and dance, covering the landscape and bringing unbridled joy after the bleakness of Oklahoma winter. But this gift seldom lasts more than a week before the yearly exodus of butterflies leaves on spring breezes.

Some friends went to the hospital to visit Christian. Though most of the butterflies had already flown away, one friend had managed to trap one for the dying boy. Christian peered at the imprisoned butterfly and then handed the jar to his mother, Marsha. "Mommy, please set him free. He's like me, in a place he doesn't like to be." Marsha opened the window, took the lid off the bottle, and let the butterfly soar away. A wistful smile crossed Christian's face. "I'm going to be like that butterfly when I fly away to Jesus in heaven."

Christian died a few days later. There are few events filled with more anguish than a child's funeral. Marsha and Gary dreaded going back to their country house filled with memories of their little boy. So their friends drove them back to the home they hadn't seen in weeks of hospital stay.

As the car turned in to the long driveway, an amazing sight awaited. The lawn was covered with a carpet of yellow butterflies. They rose by the thousands in a joyous aerial ballet. Marsha ran into their swirling midst. For several joyous moments, butterflies danced about her. She forgot her grief and began to laugh with childish delight. Then they rose en masse to catch winds to faraway places.

Grief returned as quickly as it had left, and Marsha stood alone in the yard where Christian had once played. Then a solitary butterfly returned and landed gently on her nose. It sat for several seconds, its wings gently caressing her tear-stained cheeks before flying away.

Nature has no explanation for butterflies awaiting a grieving mother two weeks after the annual migration had left. Marsha was convinced the butterfly that came back to caress her face was the one released from the hospital room. To this day, all of us are sure that we witnessed a miracle. God had orchestrated this dance of the butterflies to remind Marsha and Gary Dance of what their boy had uttered during his final days in the hospital: "I'm going to be like that butterfly and fly away to Jesus."

Did Christian know about one of nature's great miracles? When a caterpillar is ready to turn into a butterfly, it fixes itself to a branch and wriggles out of its outer skin.

Underneath is the chrysalis, which hardens to protect the insect as it transforms. It literally creates its own coffin. Then it dies, only to break out of its coffin as a butterfly destined for the heavens. It's a story of resurrection. No wonder the day Jesus rose from the dead is symbolized by butterflies. Whenever you feel like hope is gone, remember Christian Dance's story and the truth it teaches:

*If there were no death, there would be no butterflies.*

❦

It will happen in a moment, in the blink
of an eye, when the last trumpet is blown.
For when the trumpet sounds, those who
have died will be raised to live forever.

1 CORINTHIANS 15:52

# The Man Who Loved Rachel

⚬⚬⚬

No one understood disappointment better than Andy. His capacity to withstand pain was legendary. At age thirteen, he ran off to fight in the Revolutionary War. When he and his brother Robert were captured, Andy refused to shine the boots of a British officer. He was slashed across the forehead with a sword. That blow gave him a lifetime of migraine headaches.

During their imprisonment, both brothers came down with smallpox. Their mother hiked forty-five miles and somehow got her two boys released. A few days later, Robert died from the pox. Not long after Andy recovered, his mother died of cholera. He barely had time to digest her death when news came that another brother, Hugh, died of heatstroke. During that season of grief, Andy formulated a credo that would serve him well in rough years ahead: "One man with courage makes a majority."

He arose to attack life with a vengeance. When Andy wasn't fighting with local Indian tribes, he was mixing it up in barroom brawls. The hurt within drove him to inflict pain on others. Then he fell in love with Rachel. But she was a divorcée, and he had big political dreams in an age when divorce was scandalous. After he married Rachel, they discovered a court's error that meant she was still legally married to her first husband. For years afterward, Rachel was the brunt of salacious gossip. Andy fought 103 duels defending her honor. People joked that his body carried so many bullets that it shook like a bag of marbles. A bullet lodged near his heart caused coughing spasms that left his handkerchiefs soaked with blood.

But he overcame his afflictions to become a military hero in the War of 1812. He parlayed his fame into a presidential run. The stakes were great in a nation on the edge of civil war. In one of the dirtiest political campaigns in US history, his opponents portrayed Rachel as a loose woman, unfit to be the first lady. During that brutal campaign, their sixteen-year-old adopted son died of tuberculosis. Yet with toughness that earned him the nickname Old Hickory, Andy won that election in 1828. But his joy was short lived when Rachel died of an illness of the heart and lungs. A grieving Andy was sworn in at an inauguration that turned into a riot when a mob of drunken supporters trashed the White House. Newspapers gave him a new nickname: King Mob.

Andy overcame the grief of those first days to serve two terms. He managed to steer America away from the brink of civil war and wipe out the federal deficit before retiring to Nashville to live out his final years. His bloated body was racked with a persistent cough, drenching his pillows in blood. During sleepless nights, he spoke incessantly of heaven and Rachel. On his deathbed, he gasped, "I go to meet Rachel. Follow Jesus and I will see you in heaven." If you are going through a tough spell, pull out an old twenty-dollar bill. As you look at the engraving of Andrew Jackson, recall the saying that saw him through his darkest days:

***One person with courage makes a majority.***

‿◦◦◦‿

One of you routs a thousand, because the LORD your God fights for you, just as he promised.

JOSHUA 23:10, NIV

# Sources

**DAY 1: THE WOMAN WHO TORE DOWN THE WALL**

Angelo, Bonnie. *First Mothers: The Women Who Shaped the Presidents.* New York: Harper Perennial, 2001.

D'Souza, Dinesh. *Ronald Reagan: How an Ordinary Man Became an Extraordinary Leader.* New York: Free Press, 1997.

**DAY 2: A MOUSE THAT ROARED**

Hamilton, Duncan. *For the Glory: Eric Liddell's Journey from Olympic Champion to Modern Martyr.* New York: Penguin Press, 2016.

Magnusson, Sally. *The Flying Scotsman: A Biography.* New York: Quartet Books, 1981.

McCasland, David. *Eric Liddell: Pure Gold.* Grand Rapids, MI: Discovery House, 2010.

Pettinger, Tejvan. "Eric Liddell Biography." Biography Online. Last updated August 7, 2014. http://www.biographyonline.net/sport/athletics/eric-liddell.html.

**DAY 3: THE TRIUMPH OF BUBBLES**

Sills, Beverly. *Bubbles: A Self-Portrait.* New York: Bobbs-Merrill, 1976.

———. "Peter and Beverly Sills Greenough." Interview by Mike Wallace. Televised July 6, 1975, on *60 Minutes* by CBS. YouTube video, 6:21. Posted by "Beverly Sills," September 8, 2006. https://www.youtube.com/watch?v=3k Rpzn5lf0k.

Tommasini, Anthony. "Beverly Sills, All-American Diva, Is Dead at 78." *New York Times*, July 3, 2007. http://www.nytimes.com/2007/07/03/arts/music /03sills.html.

## DAY 4: THE MAN OF A MILLION LIES

Burgan, Michael. *Marco Polo: Marco Polo and the Silk Road to China.* Minneapolis: Compass Point Books, 2002.

Edwards, Mike. "Wonders and Whoppers." *Smithsonian*, July 2008. http://www.smithsonianmag.com/people-places/wonders-and-whoppers-27166/.

Polo, Marco. *The Travels.* Translated by Ronald Latham. London: Penguin Classics, 1958.

## DAY 5: WHEN FAITH WALKED ACROSS NIAGARA FALLS

Abbott, Karen. "The Daredevil of Niagara Falls." *Smithsonian*, October 18, 2011. http://www.smithsonianmag.com/history/the-daredevil-of-niagara-falls-110492884/.

CNN Wire Staff. "Daredevil Completes Walk across Niagara Falls." CNN, June 16, 2012. http://www.cnn.com/2012/06/15/us/niagara-falls-tightrope-nik-wallenda/index.html.

Hudson, Roger. "Niagara by Tightrope." *History Today* 62, no. 9 (September 2012). http://www.historytoday.com/roger-hudson/niagara-tightrope.

Thompson, Carolyn. "Nik Wallenda Faces Niagara Falls Tightrope Walk with Rich, but Tragic, Daredevil History." *National Post*, June 15, 2012. http://news.nationalpost.com/news/canada/nik-wallenda-faces-niagara-falls-tightrope-walk-with-rich-but-tragic-daredevil-history.

## DAY 6: A SHOEMAKER WHO CHANGED THE WORLD

Beck, James R. *Dorothy Carey: The Tragic and Untold Story of Mrs. William Carey.* Grand Rapids, MI: Baker, 1992.

*Christianity Today.* "William Carey." Christian History. Accessed March 6, 2017. http://www.christianitytoday.com/history/people/missionaries/william-carey.html.

Walker, F. Deaville. *William Carey: Missionary Pioneer and Statesman.* Chicago: Moody, 1951.

## DAY 7: THE DAY THE MUSIC DIED

Egan, Timothy. "Kurt Cobain, Hesitant Poet of 'Grunge Rock,' Dead at 27." *New York Times*, April 9, 1994.

Fricke, David. "100 Greatest Guitarists: David Fricke's Picks." *Rolling Stone*, December 2, 2010. http://www.rollingstone.com/music/lists/100-greatest-guitarists-of-all-time-19691231.

Marcus, Stephanie. "Courtney Love Admits to Using Heroin While Pregnant with Frances Bean Cobain." *Huffington Post*, January 28, 2015. http://www.huffingtonpost.com/2015/01/28/courtney-love-heroin-pregnant_n_6565528.html.

*Rolling Stone.* "100 Greatest Singers of All Time." December 2, 2010. http://
www.rollingstone.com/music/lists/100-greatest-singers-of-all-time
-19691231.

### DAY 8: THE DAY AN ANGEL FED ANGELS

Lewis, Jaye. "Entertaining Angels." In *Chicken Soup for Every Mom's Soul: Stories
of Love and Inspiration for Moms of All Ages,* edited by Jack Canfield, Mark
Victor Hansen, Heather McNamara, and Marci Shimoff, 150–52. Backlist,
2012.

### DAY 9: A MAP TO NOWHERE

PBS. "American Experience: *The Donner Party.*" Film resources: the diary
of Patrick Breen. Accessed March 7, 2017. http://www.pbs.org/wgbh
/americanexperience/features/primary-resources/donner-diary-patrick-breen/.
Rarick, Ethan. *Desperate Passage: The Donner Party's Perilous Journey West.* Oxford:
Oxford University Press, 2008.
Weiser, Kathy. "The Donner Party Tragedy." Legends of America. Updated April
2015. http://www.legendsofamerica.com/ca-donnerparty.html.

### DAY 10: THE WORLD'S MOST-ADMIRED WOMAN

Battle, Michael. *Practicing Reconciliation in a Violent World.* New York: Morehouse
Publishing, 2005.
Harm, Frederick R., Paul E. Robinson, Glen W. McDonald, and Harold C.
Warlick. *Sermons on the Second Readings.* Lima, OH: CSS Publishing, 2002.
Maasburg, Fr. Leo. *Mother Teresa of Calcutta: A Personal Portrait.* San Francisco:
Ignatius Press, 2011.

### DAY 11: THE MAN OF A THOUSAND FACES

Corliss, Richard. "That Old Feeling: Who Was Peter Sellers?" *Time,* February 10,
2003. http://content.time.com/time/arts/article/0,8599,421269,00.html.
Jones, Jerene. "Peter Sellers' Mask of Comedy Hid a Flawed, Spiteful Man, His
Sorrowful Children Claim." *People,* February 1, 1982. http://people.com/archive
/peter-sellers-mask-of-comedy-hid-a-flawed-spiteful-man-his-sorrowful-children
-claim-vol-17-no-4/.
North, Dan. "'There Used to Be a Me': Peter Sellers on the Muppet Show."
*Spectacular Attractions* (blog), September 26, 2008. https://drnorth.wordpress
.com/2008/09/26/there-used-to-be-a-me-peter-sellers-on-the-muppet
-show/.
*Time.* "Who Is This Man? The Many Faces of Peter Sellers." Cover story, March 3,
1980.

## DAY 12: THE TREASURE OF THE SALINAS DE SAN ANDREAS

Cool, Paul. *Salt Warriors: Insurgency on the Rio Grande*. College Station, TX: Texas A&M University Press, 2008.

SaltWorks. "History of Salt." Accessed March 7, 2017. https://www.seasalt.com/salt-101/history-of-salt.

Ward, Charles Francis. "The Salt War of San Elizario (1877)." Master's thesis, University of Texas, 1932.

## DAY 13: THE ASTERISK IN AN OBITUARY

Martin, Douglas. "Annette Funicello, 70, Dies; Beloved as Mouseketeer and a Star of Beach Movies." *New York Times*, April 8, 2013. http://www.nytimes.com/2013/04/09/movies/annette-funicello-mouseketeer-dies-at-70.html.

Moore, Frazier, and Bob Thomas. "Annette Funicello Obituary." Legacy, April 8, 2013. http://www.legacy.com/ns/annette-funicello-obituary/164132356.

Shapiro, Marc. *Annette Funicello: America's Sweetheart*. Riverdale, NY: Riverdale Avenue Books, 2013.

## DAY 14: A LETTER FROM THE BIRMINGHAM JAIL

Abernathy, Ralph David. *And the Walls Came Tumbling Down*. New York: Harper & Row, 1989.

Garrow, David J. *Bearing the Cross: Martin Luther King, Jr., and the Southern Christian Leadership Conference*. New York: William Morrow, 1986.

King, Martin Luther, Jr. "Letter from Birmingham Jail." *Christian Century* 80 (June 12, 1963): 767–73.

## DAY 15: THE SONG OF A HUMAN TRAFFICKER

Dallas, Kelsey. "Don't Mess with the Music: Why Changing Hymn Lyrics Can Be Dramatic." *Deseret News*, March 12, 2016. http://www.deseretnews.com/article/865649845/Dont-mess-with-the-music-Why-changing-hymn-lyrics-can-be-dramatic.html.

Metaxas, Eric. *Amazing Grace: William Wilberforce and the Heroic Campaign to End Slavery*. New York: HarperCollins, 2007.

Phipps, William E. *Amazing Grace in John Newton: Slave-ship Captain, Hymnwriter, and Abolitionist.* Atlanta: Mercer University Press, 2004.

Sheward, David. "The Real Story behind 'Amazing Grace.'" Biography, August 11, 2015. http://www.biography.com/news/amazing-grace-story-john-newton#!.

## DAY 16: THE CHAMBERMAID'S CHOICE

Alvarez, Alonso, Ricardo Colorado, Alejandro Monteverde, and Leo Severino. *Crescendo I*. Directed by Alonso Alvarez. Wama Films, 2011. See "Crescendo,"

YouTube video, 15:03. Posted by "MovietoMovement," October 20, 2014. https://www.youtube.com/watch?v=CafJJNETvqM.

Morris, Edmund. *Beethoven: The Universal Composer*. New York: Harper Perennial, 2010.

## DAY 17: THE FIFTEEN-MINUTE SUPERSTAR

Danger, Nick. "Superstar USA—The Meanest Show Ever." Blogcritics, May 18, 2004. http://blogcritics.org/superstar-usa-the-meanest-show-ever/.

Katner, Ben. "Superstar Jamie Squeals!" *TV Guide*, June 15, 2004. http://www.tvguide.com/news/jamie-spears-superstar-37489/.

The WB Television Network. *Superstar USA*. Episode 7, originally aired June 14, 2004. See "WB Superstar USA—Jamie—'My Heart Will Go On.'" YouTube video, 3:27. Posted by "grobisher's channel," July 31, 2009. https://www.youtube.com/watch?v=5q5u5bFatic.

## DAY 18: THE NIGHT MARS INVADED NEW JERSEY

CBS. "The War of the Worlds" (radio drama). *The Mercury Theater,* originally aired October 30, 1938. See "War of the Worlds—Original 1938 Radio Broadcasts (2011 Remastered Version)." YouTube video, 59:17. Posted by "Orchard Enterprises," February 24, 2015. https://www.youtube.com/watch?v=9q7tN7MhQ4I.

Dixon, George. "'War of the Worlds' Broadcast Causes Chaos in 1938." *Daily News*, October 29, 2015. http://www.nydailynews.com/news/national/war-worlds-broadcast-caos-1938-article-1.2406951.

*New York Times*. "Radio Listeners in Panic, Taking War Drama as Fact," headline story October 31, 1938. www.war-of-the-worlds.org/Radio/Newspapers/Oct31/NYT.html.

Schwartz, A. Brad. "Orson Welles and History's First Viral-Media Event." *Vanity Fair*, April 27, 2015. http://www.vanityfair.com/culture/2015/04/broadcast-hysteria-orson-welles-war-of-the-worlds.

Welles, Orson. "The War of the Worlds." Sacred Texts. Accessed March 7, 2017. Radio broadcast transcript of Orson Welles and Mercury Theatre on the Air in *The War of the Worlds* by H. G. Wells, October 30, 1938. http://www.sacred-texts.com/ufo/mars/wow.htm.

## DAY 19: CONCEIVED IN SHAME, BORN FOR GREATNESS

The basis of this story is found in greater detail for those willing to plow into the Yalkut HaMachiri and Sefer HaTodaah (section on Sivan and Shavuot) or Torah commentaries of Radak and Abarbanel to 1 Samuel 16:3.

Weisberg, Chana. "Nitzevet, Mother of David." *Chabad.* Accessed March 9, 2017. http://www.chabad.org/theJewishWoman/article_cdo/aid/280331/jewish /Nitzevet-Mother-of-David.htm.

## DAY 20: WHEN DOGS ROUTED A TANK DIVISION

Pile, Stephen. *The (Incomplete) Book of Failures: The Official Handbook of the Not-Terribly-Good Club of Great Britain.* Boston: E.P. Dutton, 1979.

Upton, Emily. "The Exploding Anti-Tank Dogs of World War II." *Today I Found Out* (blog), December 2, 2013. http://www.todayifoundout.com/index.php /2013/12/anti-tank-dogs-world-war-ii/#disqus_thread.

## DAY 21: THE CURSE OF THE CONTROL FREAK

Schickel, Erika. "At Zorthian Ranch, a Return to Bohemia." *LA Weekly*, July 8, 2014. http://www.laweekly.com/music/at-zorthian-ranch-a-return-to -bohemia-4832037.

*Statesville Daily Record.* "Tragedy Marks Efforts for Safety." February 12, 1948. https://www.newspapers.com/newspage/3285983/.

Swindoll, Charles R. *Man to Man.* Grand Rapids, MI: Zondervan, 1996.

## DAY 22: THE COMPASSIONATE PURITAN

*Christianity Today.* "Jonathan Edwards." Accessed March 9, 2017. http://www .christianitytoday.com/history/people/theologians/jonathan-edwards.html.

Marsden, George M. *A Short Life of Jonathan Edwards.* Grand Rapids, MI: Eerdmans, 2008.

Piper, John. "The Pastor as Theologian: Life and Ministry of Jonathan Edwards." Desiring God, April 15, 1988. www.desiringgod.org/messages/the-pastor-as -theologian.

## DAY 23: OLD WOOM'S WINNIE

Discovery. "Winston Churchill Biography." May 8, 2015. http://veday.discoveryuk .com/winston-churchill-biography/.

Johnson, Boris. "The Woman Who Made Winston Churchill." *Boris Johnson* (blog). *Telegraph*, October 12, 2014. http://www.telegraph.co.uk/news/politics /conservative/11155850/Boris-Johnson-the-woman-who-made-Winston -Churchill.html.

Kent, Richard L. "A Woman of No Importance: Elizabeth Everest." *The Tattered Remnant* (blog), December 31, 2009. http://tatteredremnants.blogspot.com /2009/09/tattered-remnants-002-elizabeth-everest.html.

Labrecque, Ellen. *Who Was Winston Churchill?* New York: Grosset & Dunlap, 2015.

## DAY 24: A RESURRECTION IN THE VALLEY OF DEATH

Richardson, Don. *Lords of the Earth*. Bloomington, MN: Bethany, 1977.

Schenk, Ruth. "Missionaries Risk All to Witness to Cannibals." Emmanuel Baptist Church. Accessed March 9, 2017. http://ib-emmanuel.org/clientimages/55879 /mission_to_cannibals.pdf.

World Team. *The Yali Story*. Directed by Dianne Becker. Rolling Shoals, 2004. See "The Yali Story (Bruno de Leeuw)." YouTube video, 27:09. Posted by "Yopi Dopi," March 9, 2015. https://www.youtube.com/watch?v=nlI9B1uGOHo.

## DAY 25: THE POSSIBILITIES AND LIMITS OF FORGIVENESS

Facing History and Ourselves. "The Sunflower Synopsis." Accessed March 10, 2017. https://www.facinghistory.org/sunflower-synopsis.

Associated Press. "Nazi Hunter Simon Wiesenthal Dies at 96." NBC News. Updated September 20, 2005. http://www.nbcnews.com/id/9404749/ns/world _news/t/nazi-hunter-simon-wiesenthal-dies/#.WMLD_jvysdU.

Simon Wiesenthal Center. "Simon Wiesenthal Biography." Accessed March 10, 2017. http://www.wiesenthal.com/site/pp.asp?c=lsKWLbPJLnF&b=4441351.

Wiesenthal, Simon. *The Sunflower*. Translated by H. A. Piehler. London: W. H. Allen, 1970.

## DAY 26: HUGS FOR THE PRESIDENT

Lavin, Cheryl. "Family Outcast: A Reagan Son Sadly Remembers Years of Neglect." *Chicago Tribune*, April 17, 1988. http://articles.chicagotribune.com/1988-04-17 /features/8803090826_1_michael-reagan-four-reagan-children-maureen.

Reagan, Michael, with Jim Denney. *Lessons My Father Taught Me*. West Palm Beach, FL: Humanix Books, 2016.

Reagan, Michael, Patti Davis, and Ron Reagan Jr. "Transcript: Reagan's Children Deliver Remarks at Service." *The Washington Post*, June 11, 2004. http://www .washingtonpost.com/wp-dyn/articles/A36014-2004Jun11.html.

## DAY 27: THE SWEET POTATO THAT DESTROYED CHINA

Mann, Charles. *1493: Uncovering the New World Columbus Created*, chapter 5. New York: Knopf, 2011.

## DAY 28: SEARCHING FOR HEAVEN

Biography. "Jackie Gleason." Accessed March 10, 2017. http://www.biography.com /people/jackie-gleason-9542440?page=4#!.

Pace, Eric. "Jackie Gleason Dies of Cancer; Comedian and Actor was 71." *New York Times*, June 25, 1987. http://www.nytimes.com/1987/06/25/obituaries/jackie -gleason-dies-of-cancer-comedian-and-actor-was-71.html.

Rich, Frank Kelly. "The Great Drunk: Lushing Large with Jackie Gleason, Part 1: The Thirsty Years." *Modern Drunkard*, February 5, 2005. www.drunkard.com /02-05-jackie-1/.

The University of Miami Library. "Spectral Collections: The Jackie Gleason Collection." Special Collections, The Mosaic, October 22, 2014. https://library .miami.edu/specialcollections/2014/10/22/spectral-collections-the-jackie -gleason-collection/.

## DAY 29: THE MIRACLE ON FLIGHT 255

Biolchini, Amy. "U-M Staff Recalls Unforgettable 'Miracle Child' on Anniversary of Deadly Flight 255 Crash." *Ann Arbor News*, August 16, 2012. http://www .annarbor.com/news/unforgettable-miracle-child-breaks-silence-for-anniversary -of-deadly-flight-255-crash/.

Flight 255 Memorial. "The Crash." Accessed March 10, 2017. http://www.flight 255memorial.com/thecrash.html.

Ryan, Scott. "Sole Survivor of Metro Airport Crash Breaks Her Silence." CBS Detroit, June 11, 2012. http://detroit.cbslocal.com/2012/06/11/sole-survivor -of-metro-airport-crash-breaks-her-silence/.

## DAY 30: THE MAN WHO CHANGED WASHINGTON

*Footnotes Since the Wilderness* (blog). "George Washington Mobilized the Monks of Ephrata for the American Revolution." Posted by "deor12," August 3, 2010. https://footnotessincethewilderness.wordpress.com/2010/08/03/george -washington-mobilized-the-monks-of-ephrata-for-the-american-revolution/.
———. "George Washington Pardons Traitor Michael Widman." Posted by "deor12," June 29, 2010. https://footnotessincethewilderness.wordpress.com /2010/07/29/george-washington-pardons-traitor-michael-widman/.

## DAY 31: THE GOOSE FROM GOOSE TOWN

*Christianity Today*. "John Huss." Accessed March 11, 2017. http://www.christianity today.com/history/people/martyrs/john-huss.html.

Poggius the Papist. *Hus the Heretic*. Ithaca, MI: AB Publishing, 1997.

Schaff, David S. *John Huss: His Life, Teachings and Death after 500 Years.* Eugene, OR: Wipf and Stock Publishers, 2001.

## DAY 32: LETTERS FROM LIZZIE

Baylor University. "The Browning Letters." Digital Collections. Accessed March 11, 2017. http://digitalcollections.baylor.edu/cdm/landingpage/collection /ab-letters.

King, Steve. "The Brownings: 'Dared and Done.'" Today in Literature. Accessed

March 11, 2017. http://www.todayinliterature.com/stories.asp?Event_Date =9/12/1846.

Markus, Julia. *Dared and Done: The Marriage of Elizabeth Barrett and Robert Browning*. New York: Knopf, 1995.

## DAY 33: THE SHIP THAT GOD COULDN'T SINK

History. "Titanic." Accessed March 11, 2017. http://www.history.com/topics /titanic.

Jeffress, Robert. *Not All Roads Lead to Heaven*, chapter 6. Grand Rapids, MI: Baker, 2016.

Mendelsohn, Daniel. "Unsinkable: Why We Can't Let Go of the Titanic." *New Yorker*, April 16, 2012. http://www.newyorker.com/magazine/2012/04 /16/unsinkable-3.

## DAY 34: GEORGE WASHINGTON'S LIAR

Creighton, Linda L. "Benedict Arnold: A Traitor, but Once a Patriot." *US News*, June 27, 2008. https://www.usnews.com/news/national/articles/2008/06/27 /benedict-arnold-a-traitor-but-once-a-patriot.

Palmer, Dave Richard. *George Washington and Benedict Arnold: A Tale of Two Patriots*. Washington, DC: Regnery, 2006.

Philbrick, Nathaniel. "Why Benedict Arnold Turned Traitor against the American Revolution." *Smithsonian* (May 2016). http://www.smithsonianmag.com /history/benedict-arnold-turned-traitor-american-revolution-180958786/.

## DAY 35: TWO MINUTES THAT CHANGED HISTORY

Conant, Sean, ed. *The Gettysburg Address: Perspectives on Lincoln's Greatest Speech*. New York: Oxford University Press, 2015.

Georgia Info. "This Day in Georgia Civil War History: December 5, 1863, Harper's Weekly Commented on Gettysburg Address." Accessed March 11, 2017. http:// georgiainfo.galileo.usg.edu/thisday/cwhistory/12/05/harpers-weekly-commented -on-gettysburg-address.

*Los Angeles Times*. "Abraham Lincoln Gettysburg Address: They Get Longer, but Not Better." Top of the Ticket: Political Commentary from the LA Times, November 19, 2010. http://latimesblogs.latimes.com/washington/2010/11/gettysburg -address-abraham-lincoln.html.

## DAY 36: THE MONSTER FROM MILWAUKEE

Ratcliff, Roy, with Lindy Adams. *Dark Journey Deep Grace: Jeffrey Dahmer's Story of Faith*. Siloam Springs, AR: Leafwood Publishers, 2006.

Ross, Bobby, Jr. "Inside Story: Did 'Jailhouse Religion' Save Jeffrey Dahmer?"

*Christian Chronicle* (August 2010). http://www.christianchronicle.org/article /did-jailhouse-religion-save-jeffrey-dahmer.

Terry, Don. "Jeffrey Dahmer, Multiple Killer, Is Bludgeoned to Death in Prison." *New York Times*, November 29, 1994. http://www.nytimes.com/1994/11/29/us /jeffrey-dahmer-multiple-killer-is-bludgeoned-to-death-in-prison.html.

### DAY 37: THE BROKEN HARPSICHORD

Lucado, Max. *When God Whispers Your Name.* Dallas: Word Publishing, 1994.

Morris, Edmund. *Beethoven: The Universal Composer.* New York: HarperCollins, 2005.

### DAY 38: THE PRICE WE PAY FOR LOVE

Lewis, C. S. *A Grief Observed.* San Francisco: Harper & Row, 1961.

Sibley, Brian. *Through the Shadowlands: The Love Story of C. S. Lewis and Joy Davidman.* Grand Rapids, MI: Revell, 2005.

### DAY 39: KISSING THE BEGGAR'S LIPS

Acocella, Joan. "Rich Man, Poor Man: The Radical Visions of St. Francis." *New Yorker*, January 14, 2013.

Englebert, Omer. *St. Francis of Assisi: A Biography.* Cincinnati, OH: Franciscan Media, 2013.

Sweeney, Jon M. "The Real Francis: How One Saint's Ancient Insights Are Transforming Today's Church." *America Magazine*, September 22, 2014. http:// www.americamagazine.org/issue/real-francis.

### DAY 40: A LIFELINE FROM THE ASYLUM

Kauffman, Barry. "The Love of God." *Hymns with a Message* (blog), January 13, 2011. http://barryshymns.blogspot.com/2011/01/love-of-god.html.

Ruffin, Mike. "Verse of Favorite Hymn Found on Wall in Insane Asylum." Devotions, February 22, 2003. http://www.devotions.com/2003/02/verse-of -favorite-hymn-found-on-wall-in-insane-asylum.html#respond.

### DAY 41: LITTLE HERBIE STEALS A QUARTER

Krebs, Brock. *Leap into History: John Dillinger in Delaware County, Indiana.* BookBaby, 2015.

Matera, Dary. *John Dillinger: The Life and Death of America's First Celebrity Criminal.* New York: Carroll & Graf Publishers, 2004.

Peters, Robert. *What Dillinger Meant to Me.* New York: Sea Horse Press, 1983.

## DAY 42: THE CINDERELLA MAN

Huntington, Brennan. *Cinderella Man: Jim Braddock - The Real Story*. Directed by Brian Gillogly and John Preston. National Geographic Documentary, 2005. See "Cinderella Man—The Real Jim Braddock Story." YouTube video, 49:35. Posted by "ibhof2," March 7, 2012. https://www.youtube.com/watch?v =Bl6ER5pwOkU.

Schaap, Jeremy. *Cinderella Man: James J. Braddock, Max Baer, and the Greatest Upset in Boxing History.* New York: Houghton Mifflin Harcourt, 2005.

## DAY 43: THE MAN WHO WAS BIGGER THAN GOD

Barlett, Donald L., and James B. Steele. *Howard Hughes: His Life and Madness*. New York: W. W. Norton and Company, 2004.

Higham, Charles. *Howard Hughes: The Secret Life*. New York: St. Martin's Griffin, 2004.

Knight, Peter, ed. *Conspiracy Theories in America: An Encyclopedia*, 1:328–30. Santa Barbara, CA: ABC-CLIO, 2003.

## DAY 44: STRONG HEART

Merrill, Mark. "The Real Story behind Valentine's Day." *Mark Merrill* (blog), February 14, 2011. http://www.markmerrill.com/the-real-story-behind -valentines-day/.

Catholic Online. "St. Valentine." Accessed March 12, 2017. http://www.catholic .org/saints/saint.php?saint_id=159.

*Wikipedia*. s.v. "Saint Valentine." Last modified March 7, 2017. https://en.wikipedia .org/wiki/Saint_Valentine.

## DAY 45: THE KING OF THE MOUNTAIN

Keith, Ted. "SI 60 Q&A: Gary Smith on Muhammad Ali, His Entourage and Memories of the Greatest." *Sports Illustrated*, October 14, 2014. http://www .si.com/boxing/2014/10/14/si-60-qa-gary-smith-muhammad-ali-entourage.

Lucado, Max. *The Applause of Heaven*, chapter 15. Nashville: Thomas Nelson, 1999.

## DAY 46: PACO'S PAPA

Elder, Robert K., Aaron Vetch, and Mark Cirino. *Hidden Hemingway: Inside the Ernest Hemingway Archives of Oak Park*. Kent, OH: Kent State University Press, 2016.

The Hemingway Resource Center. "Ernest Hemingway Biography." Accessed March 12, 2017. http://www.lostgeneration.com/.

Hemingway, Ernest. "The Capital of the World." In *The Fifth Column and the First Forty-Nine Stories*, chap. 2. New York: Scribner, 1938.

Johnson, Paul. "Hemingway: Portrait of the Artist as an Intellectual." *Commentary*, February 1, 1989. https://www.commentarymagazine.com/articles/hemingway -portrait-of-the-artist-as-an-intellectual/.

## DAY 47: THE HAND THAT ROCKS THE CRADLE

Dallimore, Arnold A. *Susanna Wesley: The Mother of John and Charles Wesley.* Grand Rapids, MI: Baker Books, 1993.

## DAY 48: THE UNWANTED BOY

Craddock, Fred B. *Craddock Stories.* Edited by Mike Graves and Richard F. Ward. St. Louis, MO: Chalice Press, 2001.

Hooper, Ben W. *Unwanted Boy: The Autobiography of Governor Ben W. Hooper.* Edited by Everett R. Boyce. Knoxville, TN: University of Tennessee Press, 1963.

Neely, Kirk H. "The Story of Ben Hooper." *Kirk H. Neely* (blog), June 8, 2009. https://kirkhneely.com/2009/06/08/the-story-of-ben-hooper/.

## DAY 49: THE GODFATHER AND THE PRIEST

Curtis, Ken. "Savonarola's Preaching Got Him Burned—1498." Christianity.com. Accessed March 12, 2017. http://www.christianity.com/church/church -history/timeline/1201-1500/savonarolas-preaching-got-him-burned-1498 -11632689.html.

Herbermann, Charles George, Edward A. Pace, Condé B. Pallen, Thomas J. Shahan, and John J. Wynne. *The Catholic Encyclopedia*, 13:190–92. New York: Encyclopedia Press, 1913.

Horsburgh, Edward Lee Stuart. *Lorenzo the Magnificent, and Florence in Her Golden Age*. London: Methuen & Company, 1908.

Martines, Lauro. *Fire in the City: Savonarola and the Struggle for the Soul of Renaissance Florence.* Oxford: Oxford University Press, 2006.

## DAY 50: THE LEPER WHO BECAME A SAINT

Catholic Online. "St. Damien of Molokai." Accessed March 12, 2017. http://www .catholic.org/saints/saint.php?saint_id=2817&+angels.

Senthilingam, Meera. "Taken from Their Families: The Dark History of Hawaii's Leprosy Colony." CNN, September 9, 2015. http://www.cnn.com/2015/09/09 /health/leprosy-kalaupapa-hawaii/index.html.

## DAY 51: A VICTORY IN DEFEAT

Frye, David. "Greco-Persian Wars: Battle of Thermopylae." HistoryNet, June 12, 2006. http://www.historynet.com/greco-persian-wars-battle-of-thermopylae.htm.

Herodotus. *The History of Herodotus*. Translated by George Rawlinson. Vol 4, bk. 7. New York: D. Appleman and Company, 1885. http://www.shsu.edu/~his_ncp /herother.html.

## DAY 52: ONE LAST SONG IN A TATTERED COAT

Songwriters Hall of Fame. "Stephen Foster Biography." Accessed March 12, 2017. http://www.songwritershalloffame.org/exhibits/bio/C10.

Swindoll, Charles R. "Insight for Today: Who Cares?" Insight for Living Ministries, July 26, 2015. http://www.insight.org/resources/daily-devotional/individual /who-cares.

## DAY 53: FROM AFRICA WITH LOVE

PBS. "The Queen of Sheba." *In Search of Myths and Heroes*. Accessed March 12, 2017. http://www.pbs.org/mythsandheroes/myths_four_sheba.html.

Women in the Bible. "The Queen of Sheba, Bible Woman." Accessed March 12, 2017. http://www.womeninthebible.net/women-bible-old-new-testaments /queen-of-sheba/.

## DAY 54: THE FOLLY OF UNNECESSARY BATTLES

HistoryNet. "Battle of Gettysburg." Accessed March 12, 2017. http://www .historynet.com/battle-of-gettysburg.

Shaara, Michael. *The Killer Angels*. New York: David McKay Publications, 1974.

Tzu, Sun. *The Art of War*. Public domain.

## DAY 55: THE DANGLING TELEPHONE

Evans, Peter. "Marilyn Monroe's Last Weekend." *Daily Mail*. Updated August 2, 2010. http://www.dailymail.co.uk/femail/article-1299496/Marilyn-Monroes -weekend--told-time-eyewitnesss-account-row-Frank-Sinatra-friends-fear -signed-death-warrant.html.

John, Elton. "Candle in the Wind." *Goodbye Yellow Brick Road*. MCA Records, 1973.

Kashner, Sam. "Marilyn and Her Monsters." *Vanity Fair*, November 2010. http:// www.vanityfair.com/culture/2010/11/marilyn-monroe-201011.

Luce, Clare Boothe. "What Really Killed Marilyn." *LIFE*, August 7, 1964.

## DAY 56: CHRISTIANITY IN SHOE LEATHER

Dorsett, Lyle W. *A Passion for Souls: The Life of D. L. Moody*. Chicago: Moody Press, 1997.

Lutzer, Erwin. "D. L. Moody: An Unlikely Servant." *Moody Church Media*. Sermon preached January 19, 2014.

M'Millen, Thomas. "Abraham Lincoln Visits Moody's Sunday School." *The Moody Church Herald*, December 1, 1908. Reproduced at The Moody Church. "Abraham Lincoln Visits Moody's Sunday School—Church History." Accessed March 12, 2017. http://www.moodychurch.org/150/teachings/abraham-lincoln -visits-moodys-sunday-school/.

Severance, Diane, and Dan Graves. "Dwight L. Moody Was Converted." Christianity .com. Last updated June 2007. http://www.christianity.com/timeline/1801-1900 /dwight-l-moody-was-converted-11630499.html.

### DAY 57: BE CAREFUL LITTLE EYES WHAT YOU SEE

Bundy, Ted. "Fatal Addiction: Ted Bundy's Final Interview." By James Dobson. Focus on the Family, 32:51. January 23, 1989. http://www.focusonthefamily .com/media/social-issues/fatal-addiction-ted-bundys-final-interview.

Michaud, Stephen G., and Hugh Aynesworth. *Ted Bundy: Conversations with a Killer.* Irving, TX: Authorlink Press, 2000.

Truesdell, Jeff. "Who Was Ted Bundy? A Look at the Serial Killer's Trail of Terror." *People*, May 12, 2016. http://people.com/crime/who-was-ted-bundy-a-look -at-the-serial-killers-trail-of-terror/.

### DAY 58: A TALE OF TWO FAMILIES

Federer, Bill. "Jonathan Edwards v. Max Jukes." The Moral Liberal, October 4, 2011. http://www.themoralliberal.com/2011/10/04/jonathan-edward-v -max-jukes/.

Fraser, Ryan. "What Legacy Are You Leaving for Your Family?" *Jackson Sun.* Updated October 11, 2014. http://www.jacksonsun.com/story/life/faith /2014/10/10/legacy-leaving-family/17054141/.

Winship, A. E. *Jukes-Edwards: A Study in Education and Heredity.* Reprint of the 1900 Harrisburg, PA, edition, Project Gutenberg, April 14, 2005. http:// archive.org/stream/jukesedwards15623gut/15623.txt.

### DAY 60: THE UNLIKELY LEADER

Hendricks, Howard, and William Hendricks. *As Iron Sharpens Iron*, chap. 4. Chicago: Moody Press, 1995.

Hyde, Douglas. *Dedication and Leadership.* South Bend, IN: University of Notre Dame Press, 1966.

Morgan, Kevin. "Obituary: Douglas Hyde." *Independent*, September 25, 1996. http://www.independent.co.uk/news/people/obituary-douglas-hyde -1365102.html.

## DAY 61: A FROG WHO MARRIED A QUEEN

*Mirror.* "Elizabeth Taylor's Former Husband Larry Fortensky Opens Up for the First Time about Their Marriage." Updated February 3, 2012. http://www.mirror. co.uk/3am/celebrity-news/elizabeth-taylors-former-husband-larry-124663.

Graham, Caroline. "She Put on a Fur Coat over Her Nightdress and Fell Giggling in the Snow: Elizabeth Taylor's Builder Ex-Husband on Their Truly Bizarre Marriage." *Daily Mail*, April 23, 2011. http://www.dailymail.co.uk/femail /article-1380014/Elizabeth-Taylors-builder-ex-husband-Larry-Fortensky-bizarre -marriage.html.

## DAY 62: SERMONS FROM THE CRYPT

Bulfinch, Thomas. *Legends of Charlemagne.* Public domain.

Holloway, April. "1,200-Year-Old Bones Found in Aachen Cathedral in Germany Believed to Belong to Charlemagne, King of the Franks." Ancient Origins, February 1, 2014. http://www.ancient-origins.net/news-history-archaeology /carlemagne-bones-found-aachen-cathedral-germany-believed-10092938.

Lucado, Max. *The Applause of Heaven*, chap. 15. Nashville: Thomas Nelson, 1999.

## DAY 63: THE MAGNIFICENT FRAUD

Lucado, Max. *The Applause of Heaven*, chap. 13. Nashville: Thomas Nelson, 1999.

History. "The Taj Mahal." Accessed March 13, 2017. http://www.history.com /topics/taj-mahal#.

*Daily News and Analysis.* "Was Mumtaz Really Buried at Taj Mahal?" August 23, 2007. http://www.dnaindia.com/india/report-was-mumtaz-really-buried -at-taj-mahal-1117182#.

## DAY 64: FAILING FORWARD

Astrum People. "Colonel Harland Sanders Biography: Inspiring History of KFC." Accessed March 13, 2017. https://astrumpeople.com/colonel-harland-sanders -biography-inspiring-history-of-kfc/.

Whitworth, William. "Kentucky-Fried." *New Yorker*, February 14, 1970. http:// www.newyorker.com/magazine/1970/02/14/kentucky-fried.

## DAY 65: SYMPHONIES AND PYRAMIDS

Johnson, Paul. *Mozart: A Life.* London: Penguin Books, 2013.

Krystek, Lee. "Khufu's Great Pyramid." Museum of Unnatural Mystery. Accessed March 13, 2017. http://www.unmuseum.org/kpyramid.htm.

Moore, Charlotte. "The Mystery of Mozart's Burial Uncovered." *Limelight*, July 10, 2013. http://www.limelightmagazine.com.au/Article/349569%2Cthe-mystery -of-mozart-s-burial-uncovered.aspx.

Nelson, David. "Mozart's Unmarked Grave." In Mozart's Footsteps, August 16, 2010. http://inmozartsfootsteps.com/122/mozarts-unmarked-grave/.

## DAY 66: THE BOY THEY CALLED SCARFACE

Chilton, Martin. "Frank Sinatra and His Violent Temper." *Telegraph*, May 14, 2016. http://www.telegraph.co.uk/music/artists/frank-sinatra-and-his-violent-temper/.

Kaplan, James. *Sinatra: The Chairman.* New York: Doubleday, 2015.

*Daily Mail.* "'Obsessive Frank Sinatra Took 12 Showers a Day and Always Smelled of Lavender,' Reveals His Widow." June 3, 2011. http://www.dailymail.co.uk /tvshowbiz/article-1392767/Obsessive-Frank-Sinatra-took-12-showers-day -smelled-lavender-reveals-widow.html.

## DAY 67: STRAW DOGS

Goodman, David Zelag, Sam Peckinpah, and Gordon M. Williams. *Straw Dogs.* Directed by Sam Peckinpah. ABC Pictures, 1971.

*Wikipedia.* s.v. "*Straw Dogs* (1971 film)." Last modified March 18, 2017. https:// en.wikipedia.org/wiki/Straw_Dogs_(1971_film).

## DAY 69: VIVA CRISTO REY!

Lopez, Kathryn Jean. "Armando Valladares, Witness to Truth." *National Review*, May 16, 2016. http://www.nationalreview.com/article/435409/castro-cub -and-resistance.

Valladares, Armando. *Against All Hope: A Memoir of Life in Castro's Gulag.* Translated by Andrew Hurley. New York: Encounter Books, 2001.

## DAY 70: THE QUADRIPLEGIC IRONMAN

"Dick & Rick Hoyt." YouTube video, 6:39. Posted by "Ironman Triathlon," February 5, 2007. https://www.youtube.com/watch?v=dDnrLv6z-mM.

Diorio, Gina L. "Inspirational Father-Son Team Dick and Rick Hoyt Race Their Last Boston Marathon." LifeNews.com, April 21, 2014. http://www.lifenews .com/2014/04/21/inspirational-father-son-team-dick-and-rick-hoyt-race-their -last-boston-marathon/.

Matson, Barbara. "Dick and Rick Hoyt Run 32nd and Last Marathon." *Boston Globe*, April 22, 2014. https://www.bostonglobe.com/sports/2014/04/22/dick -and-rick-hoyt-run-marathon-their-last-duo/0802xdlCGKe5Z84VmCgMpI /story.html.

## DAY 71: THE EXORCISM OF A SAINT

Bindra, Satinder. "Archbishop: Mother Teresa Underwent Exorcism." CNN, September 7, 2001. http://edition.cnn.com/2001/WORLD/asiapcf/south /09/04/mother.theresa.exorcism/.

Reaves, Jessica. "Did Mother Teresa Need an Exorcist?" *Time*, September 5, 2001. http://content.time.com/time/world/article/0,8599,173791,00.html.

Van Biema, David. "Mother Teresa's Crisis of Faith." *Time*, August 23, 2007. http://time.com/4126238/mother-teresas-crisis-of-faith/.

## DAY 72: LIEUTENANT BUTCH AND EASY EDDIE

Davis, John W., III. "The Murder of Al Capone's Lawyer Was Only Half the Story!" *Ruth Lilly Law Library* (blog), September 30, 2015. https://rlllblog.com/2015/09/30/the-murder-of-al-capones-lawyer-was-only-half-the-story/.

Ewing, Steve, and John B. Lundstrom. *Fateful Rendezvous: The Life of Butch O'Hare.* Annapolis: Naval Institute Press, 1997.

St. Gabriel Parish. "Easy Eddie & Butch." Accessed March 13, 2017. Modified from "Easy Eddie and His Son," Berean Publishers. http://www.stgabrielparish.com/Documents/Menu/9394.pdf.

## DAY 73: SAVING MILLY

Groopman, Jerome. "Job's Doctors." Review of *Saving Milly*, by Morton Kondracke. *New Republic*, July 2, 2001. https://newrepublic.com/article/90613/jobs-doctors.

Kondracke, Morton. *Saving Milly: Love, Politics, and Parkinson's Disease.* New York: Ballantine Publishing, 2002.

## DAY 74: THE MAN WHO DIED THREE TIMES

Friedman, Jack. "Laszlo Tokes, the Pastor Who Helped to Free Romania, Is Home." *People*, February 5, 1990. http://people.com/archive/laszlo-tokes-the-pastor-who-helped-to-free-romania-is-home-vol-33-no-5/.

Louk, Lidia. "Laszlo Tokes: The Man Who Started the Romanian Revolution." *Epoch Times*, December 16, 2014. http://www.theepochtimes.com/n3/1146036-laszlo-tokes-the-man-who-started-the-romania-romanian/.

Wax, Trevin. "How a Reformed Church Overthrew Communism in Romania." *Kingdom People* (blog). The Gospel Coalition, December 22, 2009. https://blogs.thegospelcoalition.org/trevinwax/2009/12/22/how-a-reformed-church-overthrew-communism-in-romania/.

## DAY 75: ONLY THE LONELY

Bullock, Philip Ross. *Pyotr Tchaikovsky*. London: Reaktion Books, 2016.

Greenberg, Robert. "5 (Pretty Dark) Facts about Composer Peter Tchaikovsky." Biography, May 7, 2015. http://www.biography.com/news/peter-tchaikovsky-facts-video.

Tommasini, Anthony. "The Patroness Who Made Tchaikovsky Tchaikovsky." Critic's Notebook. *New York Times*, September 2, 1998. http://www.nytimes.com/1998/09/02/arts/critic-s-notebook-the-patroness-who-made-tchaikovsky-tchaikovsky.html.

## DAY 76: THE MIRACLE AT NASEBY

Fraser, Antonia. *Cromwell: Our Chief of Men*, 154–62. St. Albans, England: Panther Books, 1975.

Trueman, C. N. "The Battle of Naseby." History Learning Site. Updated August 16, 2016. http://www.historylearningsite.co.uk/stuart-england/the-battle-of-naseby/.

## DAY 77: LET'S HEAR IT FOR THE BOLL WEEVIL

America's Story from America's Library. "The Boll Weevil Honored in Alabama: December 11, 1919." Accessed March 13, 2017. http://www.americaslibrary.gov/jb/jazz/jb_jazz_weevil_1.html.

Richardson, T. C., and Harwood P. Hinton. "Boll Weevil." In *The Portable Handbook of Texas*, edited by Roy R. Barkley and Mark F. Odintz, 696–99. Austin: Texas State Historical Association, 2000.

## DAY 78: THE RELUCTANT SPY

EyeWitness to History. "The Execution of Nathan Hale, 1776." Accessed March 13, 2017. http://www.eyewitnesstohistory.com/hale.htm.

Phelps, M. William. *Nathan Hale: The Life and Death of America's First Spy.* Lebanon, NH: University Press of New England, 2014.

## DAY 79: A MESSAGE IN A BOTTLE

Baldwin, Paul. "NASA's Voyager 2 Heads for Star Sirius . . . By Time It Arrives Humans Will Have Died Out." *Daily Express*, January 5, 2017. http://www.express.co.uk/news/world/567957/NASA-s-Voyager-2-sets-course-for-star-Sirius-by-time-it-arrives-human-race-will-be-dead.

NASA Jet Propulsion Laboratory. "What Is the Golden Record?" Voyager: the Interstellar Mission. Accessed March 13, 2017. http://voyager.jpl.nasa.gov/spacecraft/goldenrec.html.

Weber, Brandon. "A Spacecraft Launched 39 Years Ago Has Human Sounds Onboard—Now We Can Listen." Big Think, September 23, 2016. http://bigthink.com/brandon-weber/a-spacecraft-moving-at-35000-miles-per-hour-has-human-sounds-on-it-heres-how-to-listen.

## DAY 80: UNBROKEN BY FAILURE

Lincoln, Abraham. *Lincoln: Speeches and Writings 1832-1858.* Edited by Don E. Fehrenbacher. New York: Penguin, 1989.

## DAY 81: THE COUNTERFEIT ARTIST

Kaarre, Marty. "God Only Forgives People Who Are Wrong." *Story of the Day—ClimbingHigher* (blog), November 25, 2013. https://kaarre.wordpress.com/2013/11/25/god-only-forgives-people-who-are-wrong-2/.

Lewis, Dan. "The Unintentional Artist." *Now I Know* (blog), July 11, 2012. http://nowiknow.com/the-unintentional-artist/.

Stevenson, Jed. "Pastimes; Coins." *New York Times*, April 8, 1990. http://www.nytimes.com/1990/04/08/style/pastimes-coins.html.

## DAY 83: LATRODECTUS MACTANS

Forensic Outreach. "Black Widows: Four Chilling Differences between Female and Male Killers." Accessed March 14, 2017. http://forensicoutreach.com/library/black-widows-four-chilling-differences-between-female-and-male-killers/.

Strange Remains. "A Nightmare at Murder Farm: The Story of One of America's Most Prolific Serial Killers." May 18, 2014. https://strangeremains.com/2014/05/18/a-nightmare-at-murder-farm-the-story-of-one-of-americas-most-prolific-serial-killers/.

Szalay, Jessie. "Black Widow Spider Facts." Live Science, October 29, 2014. http://www.livescience.com/39919-black-widow-spiders.html.

## DAY 84: THE PRINCE OF PREACHERS

Day, Richard Ellsworth. *The Shadow of the Broad Brim*, 171–79. Valley Forge, PA: Judson Press, 1934.

Drummond, Lewis. *Spurgeon: Prince of Preachers*, 237–61. Grand Rapids, MI: Kregel, 1992.

Spurgeon, C. H. *C. H. Spurgeon Autobiography: Volume 1: The Early Years*, 527–47. Reprint. London: Banner of Truth, 1973.

## DAY 85: THEO'S BIG BROTHER

Kimmelman, Michael. "Van Gogh: The Courage & the Cunning." Review of *Van Gogh: A Power Seething*, by Julian Bell. *New York Review of Books*, February 5, 2015. http://www.nybooks.com/articles/2015/02/05/van-gogh-courage-and-cunning/.

Siegal, Nina. "Van Gogh's Pastoral Days." *New York Times*, March 12, 2015. https://www.nytimes.com/2015/03/13/arts/international/van-goghs-pastoral-days.html?_r=0.

Biography. "Vincent van Gogh." Last updated October 6, 2015. http://www.biography.com/people/vincent-van-gogh-9515695.

**DAY 86: SINGING TO JOHNNY**
Haggai, John Edmund. *My Son Johnny.* Wheaton: Tyndale House, 1978.

**DAY 87: DECISION AT TWENTY-NINE THOUSAND FEET**
Fickling, David. "Climber Left for Dead Rescued from Everest." *The Guardian*, May 29, 2006. https://www.theguardian.com/world/2006/may/29/topstories3 .mainsection.

Johnson, Richard, Bonnie Berkowitz, and Lazaro Gamio. "Scaling Everest." *Washington Post.* Updated May 12, 2016. https://www.washingtonpost.com /graphics/world/scaling-everest/.

Lauer, Matt. "Miracle on Mount Everest." Dateline NBC. Updated May 27, 2008. http://www.nbcnews.com/id/13543799/ns/dateline_nbc/t/miracle-mount -everest/#.WMi2aDsrJQI.

NBC News and News Services. "Everest Climbers Recall Near-Death Experience." NBC News. Updated June 12, 2006. http://www.nbcnews.com/id/13272568 /ns/us_news-life/t/everest-climbers-recall-near-death-experience/#.WMi5CT srJQI.

Various Climbers. "The Route." Mount Everest. Accessed March 14, 2017. http:// www.mounteverest.net/expguide/route.htm.

**DAY 89: BUTTERFLY MIRACLES**
Petterson, Robert. *Desert Crossings*, 227–31. Naples, FL: Covenant Books, 2010.

**DAY 90: THE MAN WHO LOVED RACHEL**
Andrew Jackson's Hermitage. "Orphan: Spark from the Start." Accessed March 14, 2017. http://thehermitage.com/learn/andrew-jackson/orphan/.

Burstein, Andrew. *The Passions of Andrew Jackson.* New York: Vintage Books, 2007. Kindle edition.

National First Ladies Library. "First Lady Biography: Rachel Jackson." Accessed March 14, 2017. http://www.firstladies.org/biographies/firstladies.aspx ?biography=7.

Smolkin, Rachel, and Brenna Williams. "How Jackson Tried to Save His Wife's Honor." Presidential Places. CNN. Accessed March 14, 2017. http://www.cnn .com/interactive/2015/09/politics/andrew-jackson-hermitage-history/.

# Acknowledgments

History is really *his* story. So is every chapter and line of my personal story. Sometimes the heavenly Author has chosen to insert tragedy, at other times he's sprinkled the pages with humor, and occasionally he has turned my story into a theater of the absurd. But always there is a sense of drama and excitement. Every day I jump out of bed with wonderment: *What will happen when the next page turns?* I humbly acknowledge that my Lord and Savior has designed and redeemed my life so that I might tell stories of amazing grace—not only my own, but those of thousands of others who have been woven into the breathtaking tapestry of history.

None of us walk through the pages of *his* story alone. I am indebted to Joyce Petterson, a beautiful woman of force who has sustained and supported me through a wonderful marriage and partnership. Of all my heroes, she is the superstar! I am grateful to Rachael, my attorney daughter, who challenges me to excellence and is the mother of my precious granddaughters. I am also thankful for my friend William Barnett, the president of Storytellers Creative Arts, Inc., who walks with me daily, as well as my small group of committed brothers-in-arms: Bob, John, Hal, and Carl. I am appreciative to dear friends Bob and Barbara Hattemer for allowing me to retreat to their beautiful bit of paradise on the rugged seacoast of Maine to write many of these stories. Finally, I am forever indebted to the elders, leadership, and parishioners of Covenant Church in Naples, who for fourteen years allowed me to pastor one of America's greatest congregations. Their mission across the street and around the world is truly an amazing story!

These ninety days of stories are not only amazing but also amazingly true accounts of people who have shaped our own history. It has been my intent to be as accurate as possible in both the facts and conclusions of each story. On page 271, you will find sources to further explore the backstory to each narrative.

If you have stories you would like to be told in future versions of *Amazing Stories*, or if you have feedback on any of the accounts in this collection, I would welcome your responses at robertapetterson.org.

# About the Author

Throughout his career as a speaker and author, "Dr. Bob" has carried on the time-honored tradition of storytelling, weaving unique, life-changing, and inspirational stories into all of his personal interactions with readers and fellow pilgrims.

He has served as a senior pastor at some of America's well-known churches, a counselor to community and industry leaders, and a board member of major nonprofit organizations. He was also on the adjunct faculty of Covenant Theological Seminary. As East Coast president of Mastermedia International, Dr. Bob consulted with film and TV executives in Hollywood and New York City. In addition, he has hosted numerous inspirational international pilgrimages and served as a partner with life-affirming nonprofits in their fund-raising initiatives.

Dr. Bob is in demand worldwide as a speaker and has addressed audiences across the United States and in thirty different countries. He holds both a master's and a doctoral degree. He is the author of *Desert Crossings*, *Theater of Angels*, and *Pilgrim Chronicles*.

Dr. Bob Petterson can be contacted in any of the following ways:

- Website: www.robertapetterson.org
- Facebook: www.facebook.com/Dr.BobPetterson
- Twitter: www.twitter.com/DrBobPetterson

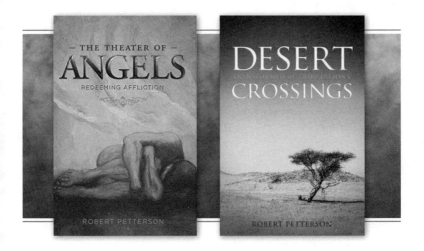